THE PEARL OF POTENTIALITY

THE PEARL OF POTENTIALITY

(Are You Ready To Catch It?)

Royal CBS Publishing, Glendora, California 91740

RCBS
ROYAL CASSETTES • BOOKS • SPEECHES
ROYAL CBS PUBLISHING

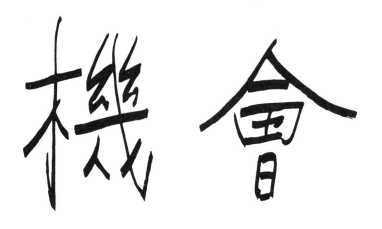

The Ancient Chinese Secret

by Dottie Walters

In the Chinese language whole words are written with a symbol. Often two completely unlike symbols when put together, have a meaning different from either of their two separate components.

An example is the symbol for "Man," and that for "Woman." When combined, they mean "Good." How wise are the Chinese.

The two symbols above stand for "Trouble," and "Gathering Crisis." When brought together, as they are here, they mean "Opportunity."

As the answers always lie in the questions, so the opportunities of life lie directly in our problems. Thomas Edison said, "There is much more Opportunity than there are people to see it."

All great leaders emerge when a crisis occurs. In the life of people of achievement we read repeatedly of terrible trouble which forced them to rise above the commonplace. Not only did they find the answers but they discovered a tremendous power within themselves. Like a ground swell far out in the ocean, this force within explodes into a mighty wave when we overcome. Then out steps the athlete, the author, the statesman, the scientist, the businessperson creating jobs for many people. David Sarnoff said, "There is plenty of security in the cemetery, I long only for opportunity."

People of achievement know this secret. The winds of adversity cannot shake them. As Charles Lummis said:

"I am bigger than anything that can happen to me.

All these things—sorrow, misfortune and suffering are outside my door.

I am in the house, and I Have The Key!"

Here is the secret of the ancient Chinese, "Hidden in trouble lies the key, our own magnificent opportunity."

Dottie Walters, Author, Speaker
President, R&D Walters Corp.,
President Hospitality Hostess Corp.,
Publisher, Royal CBS Publishing
600 West Foothill Blvd., Glendora, California 91740
(213) 335-0218

DOTTIE WALTERS
The Publisher

Dottie has shared the Platform with Dr. Norman Vincent Peale, Dr. Robert Schuller and Zig Ziglar, often as the only woman on the program. Dottie is President of Royal CBS Publishing Company, R & D Walters Real Estate Corporation and Hospitality Hostess Service, Inc., as well as being a well known author and speaker. Her book, "Never Underestimate the Selling Power of a Woman," is published by the Frederick Fell Co. of New York. Her *Success Unlimited Cassette* Album, "Selling Power of a Woman," is the first 6-hour course for saleswomen, written and narrated by a woman. SMI of Waco, Texas has found her "Seven Secrets of Selling to Women" a constant best seller. Dottie is the Publisher of "Sharing Ideas," a newsletter for Speakers. Her advertising business covers five counties in Southern California, and employs 250 people in four offices. She is the publisher of the "Success Secrets" catalog.

She has spoken across the United States many times as the featured speaker for Tupperware Inc., Beeline Fashions Inc., Home Interiors, Mary Kay Cosmetics, Amway, World Book, and many, many others. She is well known for her television and radio appearances in the United States, Canada and England, and has been featured in hundreds of daily newspapers. She is happily married and the mother of three children. Listed in Who's Who in the West, and Who's Who in American Women, she is also a member of the National Speakers Association. Dottie Walters is the author and Publisher of the new book, "SUCCESS SECRETS," How 18 Everyday Speakers Became Fortune Builders and Famous Speakers, and a new book being prepared entitled, "The Pearl of Potentiality! Are You Ready To Catch It!" The next book in preparation is "Here's Genius—the Geni-in-Us."

"THE PEARL OF POTENTIALITY: ARE YOU READY TO CATCH IT?"

By Dottie Walters

The Dragon's my Friend. He Barks and He Roars
At all thoughts of defeat or despair.
He is calling "Get Ready! Your chance is here!
My PEARL is in the Air!"

From the mists of time my Dragon has come,
Churning the darkest Sea,
As he flings in the air great PEARLS of thought
From his limitless store. For me!

And he cries as he tosses his rain of PEARLS
"Take heart! Look up! Be Free!"
The Chinese are wise. They know the PEARL'S name—
    "POTENTIALITY!"

Introduction

THE LEGEND OF THE DRAGON'S PEARL OF POTENTIALITY

by Publisher, Dottie Walters

> "What one experiences in life is the
> response of universal energy and
> intelligence to one's commands. To have
> desirable experiences, refrain from
> negativity."
> TAO

The Chinese searched the clouds and saw in their moving shapes a great friend . . . the Dragon. Since rain and good crops often followed clouds, they began to think of the Dragon as living in the sea. Then the fairy tales which wind around the Good Dragon began. His thunderous bark frightens away disease, death and bad fortune. He brings good luck to those who look for him and catch his great pearl. The very word Dragon means "Hello," "Goodbye"—"All Happiness to you," and looks like a little dragon!

Europeans have long misjudged the Dragon! The traditional picture of "Saint George Slaying the Dragon" is actually a great misunderstanding! The embattled Welsh have a dragon on their battle flags. An ancient Welsh king, "Pendragon" was the one dear Saint George slew. Shakespeare refers to "Dragonish Clouds" in Anthony and Cleopatra, while Robert Browning comes closer to the Oriental thought with his "Dragons born of rose dew, and the moon." The Dragons from the Orient are the friends of mankind.

龍

Dragon was one of the first words written down by the Ancient Chinese over 5,000 years ago. Since the Chinese were the inventors of eye glasses, printing, firecrackers, spaghetti, and a host of things the rest of the world claimed later on, the Chinese became adept at catching the Dragon's Pearl.

So, our Dragon lives in the sea. Have you noticed its churning waves? He is restless. He loves pearls, which symbolize ideas or thoughts. Our culture, too, describes "pearls of thought" and warns us not to toss them before the unappreciative.

The supply of pearls is unlimited. The Dragon is played in the Chinese New Year's parades by several men. He is larger than life! In front of him runs another man dressed as the Pearl, always jumping, running, moving from the Dragon to the people. The great colorful Dragon wags his head, opening and closing his mouth as his Pearls are tossed constantly into the air.

"Are you ready to catch it?" he thunders, "Are you?"

When you visit a Chinese restaurant, look closely at the picture of the Dragon on your plate, or embroidered in a picture on the wall. The Pearl is always shown as in movement. Sometimes it is in Dragon's claw. Sometimes in the air with little stylized wings drawn on it to indicate movement. The Chinese call the Pearl: "POTENTIALITY."

"Hidden in all small things are the possibilities of all great things," advise the Chinese. The air is full of Pearls. All we must do is look up, and put on our catcher's mitt. Hubbard said, "Thought itself is in the air." All music, invention, and philosophy were always here. The inventors merely looked *up* and visualized what was not yet, then took action.

Each of the authors in this book have caught the Dragon's Pearls. They are all successful, creative, productive. None are negative. None look down, *only up*. The Dragon's Pearl is always in the air, whizzing by our heads. Look UP! Look UP! Are you ready to catch it?

Foreword

The dragon has been a beneficent supernatural creature in Chinese mythology for centuries. Dragon-like creatures would adorn simple peasant homes to help protect against floods and they would sit atop ornate imperial palaces as well to guard against evil spirits generally. Even today, dragons are among the animal characters which line the entrance to the Ming tombs and are also to be found in the Summer Palace, the Temple of Heaven, and the Hidden City.

Long a happy symbol of the fundamentally optimistic character of the Chinese, the dragon for Dottie Walters' delightful new book is a symbol of opportunity. Better said, it is a symbol of the opportunity which comes from each of us exploring, discovering, and using the potentiality which resides within us.

I have enjoyed several careers ... as a teacher at all levels, a university division chair, a school consultant, school board member, member of the State Legislature, and Secretary of State of the largest state in the nation. My first career, as it happens, was as a dental hygienist. More recently, I have also written a little book of my own titled "The Sons of Chong."

The success I have enjoyed in each of these varied careers has come simply from the opportunity which I created for myself by discovering the potentiality within me and then "catching the pearl of potentiality" and taking it as far as it will lead.

For all who seek to make their lives as full and happy as possible, know the dragon! And know the pearl's name!

MARCH FONG EU
Secretary of State
State of California
Sacramento

March K. Eu (March Fong Eu, Secretary of State, California)

About the author: *March Fong Eu* is a highly respected and valued member of the Chinese community in the United States. She has a distinguished career in the politics of California and is presently California Secretary of State.

From the desk of a practical politician of today has come a lyrical excursion into yesterday—a fantasy, a fairy tale. In the tradition of the elusive Chinese fairy tales which have entranced readers for generations, *Sons of Chong* is a story by March K. Eu of the clash between the forces of good and evil, with the eventual punishment of evil.

March K. Eu (March Fong Eu, Secretary of State, California)

Instructions to Ordering *Sons of Chong* Are on Back Page.

Table of Contents

Finding the great in what is small, and the many in the few, repaying injury with kindness, effecting difficult things while they are easy, and managing great things in their Beginnings: This is the way.
LAO-TSZE

THE WAY TO CATCH THE DRAGON'S PEARLS

Joyce Burden
P.O. Box 5500
Lakeland, FL 33803
(813) 644-4888

JOYCE BURDEN

Set out to be the very best in your field, is a way of life with Joyce Burden. She exemplifies the rewards that come to a person who has this as a basic philosophy for success.

Today, from coast to coast, she conducts America's most popular business letter writing seminar. Her dedication to her profession is obvious to those who attend her seminars. Her abilities, coupled with her radiant personality, have catapulted her into a busy calendar schedule.

She is a graduate of Florida Southern College with a Bachelor of Science Degree in Accounting. Drawing from her management abilities, she makes time in her busy schedule to function as the Executive Director of the Billy Burden School of Memory and Attitude Incorporated.

Joyce knows the importance of results in business and the meaning of the word "profit." Her extensive background in the field of business enables her to communicate easily with others.

In addition to her many business activities, Joyce has dedicated her life to helping others find and know Jesus Christ. In this area, she is currently writing and will narrate a series of Bible stories for children.

Heaven means to be one with God.
CONFUCIUS

HOW TO REACH
BEYOND THE RAINBOW

by Joyce Burden

It was the biggest opportunity of my life! Everyone had advised me not to fly to Florida to take the test for the tax auditor position. But, I had a dream . . . I was determined to make a better life for myself and my three children, and fulfill my own potential.

Always, before anything of major *importance for me,* I talk to God. That day as I entered the U.S. Federal Building with my blood racing with excitement, I stopped, sat down in that massive lobby and told God, "You just gotta go through the interview for me, Lord. I am much too scared." Peace swept over me as I straightened up and confidently pushed the elevator button to the 7th floor.

But let me tell you how I happened to be standing there, terrified, but prayful, as that elevator door opened to great opportunities in my life.

First I found that opportunity is everywhere, and yet many find it as elusive as the end of the rainbow. Why to some is this attainment always just out of reach? And why do some individuals drift aimlessly through life never finding a purpose, not setting a goal? It is through their complacency and lack of direction that they become prisoners unto themselves. Either they wear invisible chains, shackled by someone they love and depend on, or they crouch cowardly behind their own self-made prison walls — walls that are built strong and high with restrictive words like afraid, security, or procrastination, or with fear of change and the unknown.

As women, we are often bound by the bonds our "foremothers," who were accustomed to being taken care of, set for us. They were taught to enjoy and be satisfied with their husband's station in life while they remained silent and unnoticed.

Do I sound like a feminist? Possibly, but self-value is an important state of mind and that's what I'm talking about. If I can play a part in freeing one woman from her own imprisonment or if I can signal the way towards her self-actualization, I will accept any name that applies.

Can You See It?

What you reach for in life depends to a great extent on your priorities and values. You are the extent of your imagination and your vision of yourself. For if you cannot see it, and believe you deserve it, you cannot accomplish it. A woman should neither try nor want to act or look like a man. Rather, she should expand her self-awareness and develop her superior attributes which God gave so generously to her. To be free, we must be ourselves at our very best. And being our very best should be our primary goal in life.

This is no easy task to accomplish. For to embark on such a journey, we have to break loose from our confines — which means that we must change. We must change our attitudes and our portrayal of ourselves. It is said that change is ever present, yet resisted by everyone. Many will not chance losing what little they already have on a gamble for something better. Consequently, the first thing we must do is condition our thinking to accept change.

As you begin your journey towards your ultimate goal of fulfilling your potential and thus finding the end of your rainbow, remember you will tend to be your own worst enemy. So clear your vision, open your mind, and be ready to catch opportunity when it first appears lest it pass you by, leaving you forever a prisoner of inferiority.

I have faced many seemingly unsurmountable obstacles in my life. Come along with me for awhile and let me share some of them with you.

I was born and reared in a rural community just east of a small town in north Mississippi. As the daughter of a farmer in the middle of the cotton belt, there wasn't much to do other than work. And with eight brothers and sisters, I didn't get a lot of the necessities of life and none of the luxuries.

I learned so much during those long, hot summer days. I learned how good the earth smells, how cool the summer rain feels, how cheerful the robin's song sounds, and how invigorating it is to daydream in the shade of a big oak tree when day's work is done. But I learned something more important: something I have carried with me to this day. That is—the more and harder you work, the easier work becomes; and when something is accomplished it becomes easy. Then it gives you a feeling of satisfaction and joy.

I didn't get much attention while growing up and I missed that, but I never doubted that I was loved. And my love and admiration for my mother and father, Coy and Louise Stevens, were paramount. They both worked hard and shared everything but despair. We kids could always sense the dire circumstances of the family by the gaiety or seriousness of their nightly conversations after we had been put to bed.

Satisfaction and Joy

All through high school my life centered around playing basketball. This attracted my dad's attention, and that was all the incentive I needed to give the game my best. To hold his attention, I knew I must work really hard and the lesson I had already learned was to pay off for me again. You see, I knew, that if I played hard, the game would become easy and I would know satisfaction and joy through his approval.

It was also in high school that I had my first experience with public speaking. Graduating fourth in my class, I had the privilege of making a speech at the graduation exercise. My favorite teacher told me I should seek an occupation where I could use my speaking talent. And though I had experienced a feeling unparalleled by any I had had before, I could think of no way to develop this potential. Like most girls in those days, I attended only one year of college and pursued no career before I retired to being a housewife and mother.

Unlike others, I could not bear to have my education stop here. So during almost any of those years that followed, you would find me in school working hard at one subject after the other.

Due to financial necessity, I was forced to help support my three sons—Michael, Steven, and Jeffrey. I worked as credit manager for Sears and Western Auto, and was a bookkeeper for several other companies, often on a part-time basis. I sold Stanley Home Products, going from door to door, and I later sold Avon cosmetics. I was really a successful salesperson and had top sales in my area for months in a row.

Like so many women, I also wanted a job with a regular paycheck security. I took the Government Civil Service test and was hired as a clerk-typist. In case you do not understand the Government job structure, that's the bottom of the ladder. This did not discourage me in the least because every job I had held before this did not offer the thousands of opportunities this one did. I knew I could go as far as I could dream.

Each time I got a promotion, I immediately set my goal for another one. Then I would tell myself and everyone around me, "that is my next position." I worked much harder than was required of me. But you see, I had a secret. I knew that if I worked very hard, the job would become easy and I would get that feeling of satisfaction and joy.

Reach Higher

I began my career with the IRS as a clerk-stenographer. It was the hardest job of my life because I set my goal immediately to be an auditor. Typing just got harder as I studied the tax law in my every spare moment. I worked hard but at the wrong job, and typing never got easy or fun.

After the traumatic break-up of my marriage, I had moved to Memphis. I started to work at the IRS Service Center, where there were approximately three thousand people working. And though my experience is lacking in the working conditions of a factory, this large operation appeared somewhat like a production mill with bells and buzzers governing our day. My first thought was, how do I get attention being just one pea in the bushel basket? That's what I asked my new friend who had been at her same job for 25 years. She was over 60 years old and she had no thought of reaching out for any goal except retirement. Her advice was, "You'll have to get out of here to be noticed." Knowing that to be successful, one must attract favorable attention, I could see a possible obstacle in my path. But I knew there was a way, so I began by working harder than anyone. I set definite goals and I volunteered for everything.

I faithfully reported to the accounting branch each morning at 7:30 sharp to beat the buzzer. I worked very hard, but this time for two reasons. I wanted the job to get easy and I also wanted time to think.

I have learned that I cannot make my goals come true if I don't take time to think about them. I still wanted to be a tax auditor. I didn't have the educational requirements, so as usual, I was attending night classes trying to obtain them.

Think-Plan-Ask

While thinking, planning, and asking questions, I found that the Government has a college equivalency test called FSEE. If I could pass it, I would be educationally qualified. I took the test and passed! I immediately sent applications all over the country. In one day I mailed thirty-five. I wanted that job and I knew someone would want me. I was told it would be impossible as this was one of the most competitive jobs in government. But I knew I could do it, and I reached out for what I believed could be mine.

The power of the universe comes only through the hand of God. It would be accurate to refer to myself as "we" for I never undertake any task without His help and guidance. He clearly states in Matthew 17:20: "If ye have faith as a grain of mustard seed, . . . nothing shall be impossible unto you." I go even a step further; I take Him with me everywhere. We are always successful!

God was with me once again and I received a call to come in for an interview for a tax auditor. But there was a condition. I must pay my own expenses and fly to Florida with no assurance I would get the job. Other applicants, who must have had better qualifications than I, were sent to interviews at the expense of the government. So from everyone I asked, the advice was the same, "Don't go."

Reach Out!

But the voice inside me shouted, "Reach out for the impossible!" for to obtain anything less, takes the joy and pride of accomplishment away. So with borrowed money, faith in God, and determination, I left for that fateful interview in Florida. Needless to say, God did a great job, and I was told that day to report to tax school in two weeks! My children and I hurriedly packed and we were off to a new adventure, a great *opportunity*.

No sooner was I through training, than I saw something else I liked even better. That was to become a Federal Agent. The Internal Revenue Agents get to work outside the office, auditing the big corporations. To me, this appeared to be the ultimate challenge. The qualifications, however, included a Bachelor's degree in accounting — with no exceptions. Few women ever got the job. I don't know the percentage that did, but I'll guess about two percent. Many offices had no women at all.

I started to night school in a really serious way. I'm a firm believer that you must prepare yourself for your goals. If you do not want to go back to school, it doesn't mean you cannot reach your goals in life, but each of us must be realistic. And realistically, the goal I reached for had an educational requirement. I would never let anything so attainable keep me from achieving something I want, and neither should you.

Another Pearl of Potentiality!

Months passed. Then, unexpectedly, a position for agent came open in my office, and I still lacked twelve semester hours having enough credits to obtain my accounting degree. What a trauma! There were fifteen agents, all men, and the turn-over was slow. It would take another six months to get the college degree I had to have. I applied anyway. Again the impossible, but why not? I had seen the impossible done before and it could be done again.

I wrote on my application that I had a BS Degree in accounting—as of May, six months away. I said a little prayer, kissed the application for additional luck, and sent it on its way. Then I "dubbed" the position. That means I told everyone the job was mine. When talking to the agents, I would say, "When I get over there in my new job. . . ." And I started cleaning out my desk and telling my colleagues goodbye. Before long everyone was referring to it as Joyce's position, and I knew I had succeeded in organizing a mental power towards my goal.

One day I was bragging about my new job to the manager from the district office. He candidly told me I was probably going to be disappointed. He said that competition was tough, that there were many young men just graduating from college who had applied, as well as men who had previously worked as agents and for one reason or another wanted to come back. More important—he was to be on the interview panel.

The big day for the interview finally came. I cannot stress to you too much the importance my faith in divine guidance plays in helping me to reach the impossible goals in my life.

Let Go and Let God

I admit to God that I am incapable of controlling the interview. I tell Him to control my mind, my actions, and the words I say. I believe with all my heart He will do and say exactly the right thing. If you are trying to get a promotion of any kind in the business world today, you must master the art of interview. I know my way works and I beg you to try it.

It was a pressure interview. I had to sit in front of a panel of six men and respond to their questions. I later found out that excessive pressure was put on me to see how a woman would react under stress. I was disappointed because I was treated differently and because there were no women on the interview panel. I left the room that day angry and disillusioned, knowing I was not selected.

Only Believe

It was over a week before I heard anything, and during all this time I felt all the humiliation of defeat. Those who had believed in me were disappointed too. Not one laughed at me for having believed the job was mine.

It was a beautiful day when I found out the job was mine! Thinking I had lost, made victory even sweeter. I had reached the summit of success. At last I knew how it felt to reach beyond the rainbow. I loved every day I worked. The challenges I craved were always there and when you are the only female agent with fourteen male agents, you have to be better just to be as good. I must say I never tried to act like a man or ask that I be treated like one. I am proud to be a woman and I want to look, act, and feel like one. I want people with whom I do business to respect my mental capabilities and to accept me as the person I am.

Change Is Inevitable

Life is constantly changing, and about this time circumstances were developing towards a change in mine. I met, fell madly in love with, and married my husband, Billy Burden. Billy is America's foremost memory training expert and has for many years traveled continuously across America teaching his memory seminars.

From the first day we met we have tried to spend as much time together as possible but never enough to satisfy either of us.

Then when my son, Steve, decided to go to college in Mississippi that September, Billy and I began to plan how we could be together all the time. The idea created a real dilemma for me, however, as it would mean giving up the job I had worked towards for nearly ten years, the job which furnished me a feeling of security and independence. And since I had worked hard, the job had become easy, giving me that grand old feeling of satisfaction and joy.

This need for security was just one of the words of my prison wall, and the struggle with myself was gigantic. Night after night, I tossed and turned in restless sleep. I imagined by day and dreamed all night about how life would be if I made this drastic change into a new and uncertain world. Conversely, I tried to imagine how it would be on those long weeks when I would be completely alone. Billy insisted that the final decision had to be mine.

One morning I woke up and my mind was clear. What a relief! I had made my decision and I promised myself I would never look back.

What You Can Imagine?

I believe you become the product of what you imagine and what you think about all day. The conclusion I came to was the result of my inner debates and thinking. The decision was that I should make the change, and change I did.

There were moments when doubt crept back across my mind, and I could have begun the battle with myself all over again. But being a decisive person brings you a step closer to being a dependable person, so I quickly replaced these doubts with beautiful visions of my new life. My dreams grew so vivid and exciting that anticipation to get going on my new journey was foremost in my mind.

But the change was even greater than I expected. I fought for my self-reliance and self-esteem. My husband, like many husbands, had no confidence in my business abilities. He wasn't sure I could make out a bank deposit slip correctly. How could this be happening to me? Holder of a degree in accounting, competent auditor of large corporations, and my husband didn't trust me to fill out a deposit slip.

I cried in my self-pity and mentally digressed to the position I know many wives digress to. I wanted to share his career and his life, yet he wasn't accustomed to sharing and I feared I had failed.

Look Up!

I could give up and go back to my old career. But going back is never the direction I want to pursue. Life and time march always forward and if we are to conquer our dreams, it will be done by aiming straight ahead. That was the day my new goals broke from the clouds and took their proper place of priority.

I began by getting up early each morning. I tackled each day with a new interest and enthusiasm and I involved myself in every aspect of our business. I worked hard at proving myself a capable business partner, possibly harder than I ever had to do with anyone else. But our love and respect for each other were strong and we were soon each other's best friend and confidant.

Billy was the first to notice I had potential as a writer. He encouraged me in every aspect of it. I must admit I have always had a secret desire to write a novel that would stand with the greats of all time, and I know it is only a matter of time before I do so, because I can visualize it.

I was soon taking a notebook with me everywhere. I wrote on planes, in airports, in hotel lobbies, in restaurants, in libraries, and in the park on Sunday afternoons. I wrote articles and stories of all kinds and on all subjects. I sent them to many publishers, sometimes knowing they did not accept unsolicited material. I knew that if I sent enough, I would get the attention I wanted and someone would publish my work. And just as I knew it would happen, my articles began to be accepted.

Write It Right

Additionally, I pondered on an area of need I had discovered during my years of working and succeeding in the business world. I found that many people fall short of success simply because they cannot properly translate their ideas into words when they try to communicate by letter. I spent many long months creating a course on business letter writing. The research was a demanding and tiring experience but it was effort well spent. Now I teach seminars on this subject all around the country. Through this teaching I discovered a new feeling of fulfillment. It is one that comes with being able to help others accomplish their goals.

When I first began to write, it was hard to visualize all the avenues open to me. Every day it seems there is something new that needs to be written. As an example, there is a special area of writing where Billy and I have found we share equal enthusiasm. He writes the music and I write the lyrics to gospel songs. Many of these have already been recorded in a religious album.

I have found that the journey through life is nothing more or less than the experiences we encounter. The more varied the experiences, the greater the opportunity to fulfill our potential. I know now that every change in our lives should be tackled with optimism and with a desire to search out a new awakening inside ourselves. I was so sure I had found my niche in life that I resisted change. Then I discovered something better and more alive. I will never close the door to opportunity again nor will I ever set or limit my potentials.

I have learned that *opportunity is everywhere,* and I have learned the value of balancing the priorities of my life. I have God for my anchor and mainstay, I have a wonderful husband to love and share life with, and I have good children to be proud of.

To you who are reading this book, I reach out my hand. From where you are—stand up—reach out—and *catch your "Pearl of Potentiality."* Whichever direction you travel on your journey through life, keep a vigilant watch ever searching for the opportunity to change into the person God intended you to be from the beginning. For only when you've *developed your potential to its fullest,* will you know true freedom—the freedom that comes when you know how to reach for the end of the rainbow and beyond.

Joyce Nemeth
410 Tenth Avenue
San Diego, CA 92101
(714) 236-9414

JOYCE NEMETH

What does a 35 year old mother of two, world acclaimed tattoo artist and corporate executive all have in common? The answer is Joyce Nemeth, President of the tremendously successful self-named company, Tatoos by Joyce, Inc.

Graduating from Wayne University with a degree in Art Education, Joyce was married to a medical student and taught elementary school for four years. Finding the job and that type of life unchallenging enough for her exuberant and aspiring personality, she quit teaching and soon came to San Diego with her family. Coming from a family that had been tattooing for two generations and learning the ancient body ink art from her grandfather on Coney Island many years before, Joyce recognized the need for a tattoo artist that catered especially to women. So, in September, 1976 she opened her plush 5th Avenue tattoo shop in San Diego.

"People have always had an urge to adorn their bodies but most just cannot cope with the permanence of a real tattoo," says Joyce. Thus began for her one of the most successful and fulfilling ventures of her life: to manufacture a removable tattoo.

As the product took off in the retail market, so did Joyce's career. As President of Tatoos by Joyce, Inc. she has become a worldwide celebrity. She has traveled extensively all over the world doing television talk shows, radio spots, magazine interviews and promotions of all kinds. Today she is one of a few successful women who have their own million dollar corporation.

Human nature is innately creative. By devotion to the spirit within, a person awakens to the intuitive impulses which lead one to expressions of creativity.
TAO

THE MILLION DOLLAR TATTOO

by Joyce Nemeth

Four years ago I decided that I wanted to change the entire course of my life, and go forward toward a new goal. My goal was to be rich and famous in five years. Today, four short years later, I am the President of Tatoos by Joyce, Inc., a manufacturing company that has grossed over 1 million dollars its first year; I have traveled across the world to places as far away as Australia and New Zealand, I have been on national T.V. talk shows throughout the U.S. and abroad, had dozens of magazine and newspaper articles written about me. I personally know many famous celebrities and presidents of multi-million dollar corporations that I would have been terrified to speak to just a few short years ago. How did all this happen, and happen so quickly? It is going to be my greatest pleasure to tell you, in the hope of inspiring and motivating all of you to discover your potential and achieve it as I feel I have done. I know there are thousands of you out there that consider yourselves quite ordinary, but I also know that many of you can become quite extra ordinary. I am going to tell you just how I did it so that in a few short years I will have the extreme pleasure of hearing from some of you that were motivated by my story. I know I will hear from you because the potential is there for many of you: go after it, you can do it, I know you can! The following is a detailed account of how I did it. I don't intend for you to copy my actions exactly, but only to follow the steps and apply them to your own ideas.

The Crucial First Step—Be Positive, Even if It's Killing You.

The first and most important thing I did was to take a good look at myself and to make a list of my strongest and weakest points. I decided that once I had listed and accepted my strengths and weaknesses, I could then make some assumptions about the possibilities that existed for me. I had never put down in black and white the real truth about myself and it was really very sobering. I found I had an incredible amount of weaknesses: but I decided to take my few strongest points and to use them to their fullest advantage. I was going to make such an extra ordinary effort to make the most with my best points that they would far out-shadow my weaker ones.

At this crucial point, I began to have some doubts; there were so many weak points and I felt so fragile, so I did what was necessary; I made up my mind that I would be totally positive. I would not listen to anybody that would not encourage me. I completely ignored any discouraging remarks. I intended to succeed. I was going to do it. I would not even allow myself to doubt it for a minute. If anything I did failed, I would immediately accept it, pull myself together, devise an alternate plan and go forward once again. At first, I had to make a conscious effort to be so positive all the time. But soon, I started having small successes, and with each success, I became more and more positive until finally I began to feel that I really could and would do anything that I set out to do. I was on my way. As far as I was concerned, there was no stopping me. I ate, slept, and breathed my success goal: *I was going to make it, no other thought was acceptable. This kind of positive attitude is absolutely essential!* You must believe you will succeed and if your goal is one that you can realistically accomplish, based on your known physical and mental abilities, you will succeed. It is the emotional side of you that can get in the way and cause you to doubt. Do not allow this to happen.

Uniqueness . . . The Key To Recognition.

I decided very early in this new phase of my life that it would be better to become famous first and rich later, rather than vice versa. I knew that from fame would spring some opportunity to become wealthy but not necessarily the other way around. Why not go for the whole thing? Why settle for less than the full shot?

I knew I had to begin with some skill I had, no matter how unused or how unproven that skill had been, and I knew that I had to do something extremely unique with this skill because I was going to need lots of publicity and recognition to put part 1 (fame) of my plan into action and uniqueness was the key. I pondered this for several months until one morning I woke up with a start; it had hit me like a bolt of lightning. I had thought about and rejected several ideas and decided against each one of them as not being the right one, when to my delight, I knew I finally had it. I was going to become a tattoo artist. My grandfather had been a tattoo artist many years ago and as a teenager I spent some time in his shop learning the art, but never for a moment had I considered doing such a thing for a living. But this was not going to be just a living. I was going to do something so different with this skill that people everywhere would be interested and the media would just love it. I would make my shop and myself so interesting that the publicity I wanted would come easily. I felt certain that it would work and it did. I knew that I was the farthest thing from the public's image of the average tattoo artist and that I could capitalize on this and make my business and myself completely unique.

I decided to open up the only tattoo shop of its kind in the world and I proceeded to make sure that every local T.V. station and newspaper knew about it. My shop was going to be like a fancy boutique or beauty shop. Beautiful carpeting, plants everywhere, classical music playing on the stereo. I would cater to women and work strictly by appointment. Every customer would receive a custom designed tattoo. I would never do the same one twice. My initial investment had to be minimal, so I searched for a run down place with great potential. I convinced my landlord to pay for half of the carpeting and improvements and I decorated the place by searching garage sales for bargains. While I was doing all this, I practiced and polished my tattooing skill by touching up tattoos on sailors that didn't want to spend money in a real tattoo shop. I worked for minimal fees knowing it would pay off in the future. I tattooed almost anyone that asked me. I worked with my clients on my dining room table hoping the local health department wouldn't find out about it. The circumstances were far from comfortable. I had two pre-schoolers and two enormous dogs wandering in and out at all times, but I was so excited with my plan that I refused to be daunted. It was as if I had on blinders. I could only see that light ahead that I knew was there and I was actively moving forward in a positive direction. I was getting "higher and higher on life" with each passing day.

The big day finally arrived. Everything was ready, including me. I had beautiful business cards printed up. The cards were adorned with an extremely sophisticated woman wearing a delicate red rose tattoo on her shoulder. I intended for there to be no doubt in anybody's mind when they saw my business cards that I ran a very fancy place. I walked over every square foot of the local universities and tacked my cards on every bulletin board that I could find. Very soon it started to happen; the phone began to ring; the customers were coming: I was in business!

One Step At a Time . . . It Will Start To Happen . . . Like Magic!

It was time for step 2. I typed up a letter explaining all about myself, my unique skill and unusual shop and I personally took it around and handed it to several different people at every local television station and newspaper. I made sure that I met the news people personally and that I looked as sophisticated as possible so as to make a lasting impression on these people. They probably would otherwise have assumed that I looked like a typical motorcycle gang member. It worked! They couldn't believe that I was a real tattoo artist and that my customers were not only women, but professional people, housewives and university students. Within a month I received a four-column article in a local business paper and a three-minute spot on the local news. And then I found out that when you're really unique the media gets very hot! The first year I had over two dozen major newspaper articles and was on local and national news at least a half a dozen times. Business was good, I was making a living. I had become a minor celebrity. It was time to move on to the next step.

Step 3 was crucial. If I was going to succeed in the business world I needed to associate with business people that would be knowledgeable of what was happening. I had never been a joiner. I did not like clubs or organized groups, but I overcame this and joined every local business group I could find. I went to breakfast club meetings and lectures and talked to everyone I could talk to. I was hungry for knowledge. Before long I found myself being drawn to a particular group of people that I had not even known existed before. They were called Entrepreneurs, a

varied and unusual assortment of people that fit no particular mold as far as age, sex, physical appearance, etc.
except that they had all accepted the basic premise that
there was always a way to make a good living and often
even get rich without ever working for anybody else.
These people often went into a new venture every year or
so, or several at one time, and they all had one thing in
common: *the complete and total confidence that the only
basic thing one needs to succeed in business is a creative
idea and the ability to convince others of the value and
worth of these ideas and success will naturally follow.* They
consciously knew what I unconsciously had known all
along. What a revelation! My second electric bolt! I knew
now it was only a matter of time until I had the big idea. In
the mean time I would prepare myself so that when that
idea struck I would be ready.

How Not to Miss Your Big Chance . . . Be Prepared!

I had already taken care of several of the necessary
steps of preparation. I had acquired a skill that would take
care of my immediate financial needs and daily living
expenses and allow me some free time to pursue my new
idea when it occurred. I had acquired many business acquaintances that I could call upon for sound advice or to
bounce my ideas off, I had made a conscientious effort to
improve my physical and mental health by diligently
working on my eating habits and physical exercise program. I knew a great deal of physical and emotional
strength would be required to support the energy level
necessary for my yet unknown entrepreneureal venture.
The final step was to make sure I had an excellent and
personal relationship with a bank. *Financing would be a
key issue one day in the future.* I took out a small loan and
paid it back in a short time. I proceeded to take out several
more loans with other banks and diligently paid them
back on time or sooner. At the same time I would regularly

stop in at each of these banks and drop off copies of recent news articles, or give the news of an upcoming T.V. appearance to my loan officer. I made personal friends with all the bank tellers and kept them advised of my publicity. I was becoming known by my bankers as a local celebrity and I knew that this little bit of personal dazzle would pay off. They came to consider me as a person of tremendous energy and vitality and when the time came and I really needed them, they were psychologically in my corner. I knew that if I didn't have a valid reason to qualify for help from my bankers, I could probably have done my entire dazzle routine including a tap dance on their desks and it wouldn't have helped, but I had learned a well kept secret . . . bankers are human just like the rest of us and their emotions can often play an important part in influencing their decisions. I was never to forget how important it was to set up a very special rapport with people I might need to help me in the future. The most important thing I tried to remember was to *be sincere.* I was truly beginning to see myself as an extra-ordinary person and I wanted to make sure that everyone I was involved with saw me that way also. I sincerely believed in what I was doing and everybody knew it.

One day a writer from a magazine came to interview me and told me about some removable tattoos that she used to buy in New York City several years ago. She said that everyone she knew wore them and that they had been written about in Playboy Magazine. She was a very "with it" young woman and if everyone she knew had bought them they must have been a pretty big fad. Bingo! That was it! I would manufacture removable tattoos and sell millions of them. I knew I had the big idea I was waiting for! Now I am sure that if I had not done all the things I have been telling you about to prepare for this big event, I probably would have let this fantastic idea go right by me and never have recognized it. I am sure we all have had some excellent ideas but were not in a position to act upon them. I had made sure I would be ready to act and I was.

How to Make Sure You Are the "Boss"

My first step was to establish a team to help me as I had never been involved with production or manufacturing of any kind and I obviously could not do it all alone. However, I felt strongly that it was my idea, I was the creative force and I would always remain in control. I would allow others to share in my idea in exchange for their services or talents but I would never relinquish the directing force. I immediately went to see an attorney, specializing in businesses, to find out all the ways that I could structure my new business and always assure my controlling it. He explained all about partnerships, corporations, etc. and *advised me to incorporate* just as soon as I could and to always retain a majority of the stock. This was some of the best advice I have ever been given. So many people end up dealing from a position of weakness and I was going to make sure I would always be dealing with any business associates from a position of strength. What a crucial and important lesson that was! Many times I have been in the position of having to make crucial decisions affecting my future and the future of my business. The knowledge that I have the ultimate power to *make these decisions affecting me* makes everything so much cleaner, simpler and more conducive to my mental and emotional health.

How To Get Others To Help You . . .
    And Have Them Loving It!

To pull my story together, I selected two partners out of the many people I knew. One person to handle production of my product and one person to handle the legal and financial aspects of the business. I consistently called upon everybody I knew for assistance. Nobody ever turned me down. One person led to another and I soon found I had a fairly extensive network of advisers. If I had a marketing problem, I called someone that had been recommended to me with knowledge in this area. If I needed some publicity advice, I called someone with that knowledge. Many people have asked me how did I get so many people to help me and give me all this wonderful knowledge and advice.

Why were so many people so eager to do so much for me? It all relates back to a *few basic principles that I learned in the very beginning.* Firstly, enthusiasm is extremely contagious! I was so enthusiastic about what I was doing that most people were actually enjoying doing things for me because my project was so exciting and so much fun. Nobody ever felt that they were putting themselves out with no return. The enjoyment they were getting out of helping was their return. Secondly, most people are afraid of being taken advantage of, and are therefore very careful about extending themselves. I was totally sincere in my requests. I would never have considered using any knowledge I was acquiring to do anything in the slightest way dishonest or unethical and I was totally sincere in my desire to extend myself in return, in any way that I could, to anyone that had helped me. I told this to all of my friends and business acquaintances and took every possible opportunity available to do things that would prove my sincerity. This kind of attitude soon attracted many people who not only helped me while I was on my way, but whom I consider today to be my true, good friends and vice versa.

The Best is Yet to Come!

And the best is yet to come! Now that I have achieved my goals, I no longer feel so driven. The world has opened up for me and I now see dozens of new opportunities and directions that I may choose to take. Although I have truly given one hundred percent of my mental, physical, and emotional energy to achieving what many people thought were impossible pipe dreams, I do not regret one moment of it, no matter how exhausted I may sometimes have felt, because I now know that what most ordinary people consider the impossible is very, very possible. The secret is not to be ordinary . . . the whole world and all its potential is there to be taken by those who know that they can have it all . . . *they need just to reach out for it and never stop until they get it.*

Anita Faye Davis
1105 W. Francisquito
West Covina, CA 91790
(213) 961-1007

ANITA FAYE DAVIS

Anita Davis is a Diesel Electric Locomotive Engineperson the first for the Santa Fe Railway in Southern California.

She is currently working out of the Los Angeles Hobart Yard Los Angeles Terminal Division, Coast Lines.

To the children for whom she has presented motivational as well as safety talks, she is "Annie Engineer".

To the children along the tracks, she is a smile and wave of the hand.

For three years following her divorce in 1969, she attended college in the evening; supporting herself and her two small boys by working as a Teacher's Aid during the school months and a zoo attendant in the summer.

Through adversity and success she has been supported by her sons, Suede Lee, twelve and Benjie, ten.

Anita and her "crew" live with her sister in their five-bedroom home in West Covina, California.

She has been interviewed by local newspapers and television including Channel Seven's special on sexual harassment on the job with Inez Pedrosa.

A member of the National Organization for Women and a firm believer in the ability that lies within all women, she is currently entering a career in public speaking in an effort to share encouragement and direction for those looking for something more.

"In all things success depends on preparation. Without such preparation there is sure to be failure!"
CONFUCIUS

Only One Potty
On the Choo-Choo?

by Anita Davis

"Santa Fe caboose 460 to engine 8737, you have a good air brake test; your conductor is on board and ready to go."

"Santa Fe engine 8737 to Hobart Tower; this is the Extra Habor train ready to leave off track 16. May we have the line-up?"

"Hobart Tower to the Extra Harbor, you have the line-up, highball . . . and have a good trip, Anita."

"8737 to Conductor Peaches, we have a *'Green Block Signal.'* Here we go."

"Caboose 460 to engine 8737; *all moving."*

Indeed my "train" is moving on a *"Green Block Signal!"*

How did I get my "train of success" together, becoming a female Railroad Engineer? How do you get your "train" together and over the road to the station at the end of the line?

There are six mileposts that have never failed to get me there.

Called On Duty

September, 1974 as my fingers paused over the keys to the antiquated, black Royal typewriter, the bain of the clerks in the freight car repair department (Rip track), my eyes rested on the slow determined movements of one of the small blue and yellow engines used in Santa Fe's local yard. Through the slats of the window blinds I watched it run on a tapestry of steel rails glistening from the falling night-time mist. It was patiently guided by the tiny lanterns of its three-man switch crew: a circle of the lantern to back up, a vertical up and down movement to go forward, a big "u" to stop. Backward, forward, stop; backward, forward, stop; shoving freight cars in and out of tracks, making the trains which the big powers, those engines that pull eleven thousand-ton trains over mountains would take to other towns, other states, even other countries.

This scene, my dissatisfaction with mere existence and the staccato blare of Santa Fe's road radio, barking mysterious yet fascinating messages to that and other engines was the beginning of the "Train of Success" I was to build in my life.

To my knowledge at that time there were no women Engineers or Switchmen. I asked questions about operating a locomotive, what type of training is given, what are the physical requirements, the work conditions? etc. Every answer I received only confirmed my belief that I, a woman, could handle the job effectively. I continued combing the minds of everyone who had information that would help me reach my goal, how do the signal lights work and what do they mean? What is a "wye", how much does a coupler weigh, what stops the train?

To become an Engineer was soon the one thing in my life I wanted, I had to have! I allowed myself no doubts, for I feel them to be the seeds of failure.

I kept in constant touch with those who would do the hiring, by writing again and again always with the positive approach that what they had in me was a good employee. They needed good Engineers, therefore, they needed me.

November 1974, I was at the Rip track working with the telex and monitoring the yard radio. Interviewing me for possible transfer to engine service was a red-neck railroader from the steam engine days. While answering questions about why I wanted to be an engineer and whether or not I understood the responsibilities of that job, I was stopped mid-sentence by a question I shall never forget.

"Ah, mam, do you realize there is only one potty on the choo-choo?"

"Why yes, that seems sufficient."

"Well, ah, do you realize these potty doors are sometimes emergency exits and cannot be locked?"

"No, I didn't know that."

"Well, really miss, I mean, ah, what would you do if someone, you know, walked in on you while using it?"

"Say, 'Hi'!"

My interviewer could not see beyond his curtain of traditional ideas. A woman on the engine?? But there is only one potty on the choo-choo! Is there? Yes, but then, there is only one engineer on the train.

November 5, 1977, I grabbed the throttle of engine 2504 as Santa Fe's first woman engineer in Southern California.

Milepost 1

Look up from your desk of mere existence. Look out the window of your mind and see the opportunities falling like pearls. Determine to grab the throttle and hold tight.

Train Orders, Bulletins & Block Signals

No Engineperson, including myself, takes hold of the throttle without considerable preparation. Having been 'called on duty', I know my final destination, but between here and there lies miles of track and I must know every detail of that road. I read the bulletins (posted information concerning that and other areas), the timetable (a schedule of information in pamphlet form, giving passenger train station times, the milepost location of stations and much more), my train orders (messages given for each trip often concerning temporary restrictions) and know my block signals, (those magic lights of red, yellow and green that guide me to my destination). In short, I plan ahead. I visualize my trip from departure to arrival.

Milepost 2

Prepare. Know where you are truly going. Be well informed. Plan ahead every mile of the way from start to finish.

Highball On the Air

Part of my preparation before every trip is to make equipment checks. I check to see if my gauges, air, fuel, oil, water, air pressure, all show correct readings. There must be the proper supplies, road flares, red flag and warning torpedoes. The electrical cables must be properly secured for correct "on line" operation. Do my pneumatic air controls function properly? They must. That compressed air is the muscle behind the brakes as well as the lungs of the whistle and horn.

Even a visual inspection must be made. If there are flat spots on the wheels they will not roll smoothly and could even be hazardous on the road. The headlight must shine brightly for the train to be seen.

February 1978, I had received a late call from the crew office and was to be the Engineer at one of the outlying stations in the Los Angeles area. This road job was to deliver to and pull from industries in that area along the main line. Being Saturday, the crew would want to get the work done as fast as possible and go home. The engine I was to use had been set out by another train along with two other smaller engines. A very brief glance showed my engine to be 'cut off' from the other two and as it was not customary to leave an engine standing without air controls operational. I failed to check the position of the valves, besides, I was in a hurry, I wanted to please my crew. I climbed the steps at the front of the engine, "knocked off" (released) the hand brake, a manually operated chain-and-lever device and entered the locomotive cab. Giving a brief glance over the gauges, I adjusted the sideview mirror, pushed the "generator field" switch to power position, shoved the reverser handle into the control stand and positioned it for forward movement. To get the engine moving, I brought the throttle out to its minimum power position, 'run one', and immediately shut off again, as I was on a downhill grade and only wanted to get the engine rolling enough to test the brakes.

My surprise, when I grabbed the controls for the brakes and got no braking force, could only be matched by my terror of the red signal light ahead of me or hitting the "d"-rail also on the track ahead. To go by the first would mean immediate suspension from my job; the second would put the engine on the ground.

The engine rolling down the track was picking up speed and I had no way to stop it. Or did I?

Clutching the jack-like handle of the manual brake with both hands and all my one hundred and twelve pounds I pumped up and down, up and down until through the hot shining sun, the sweat of determination and the damp, stringy mass of my red hair I could see the engine's movement stop.

I have never since failed to make a thorough inspection.

Milepost 3

Make an inspection. If you have "flat spots" in your appearance they make the rolling rougher. If you have an 'on-line' attitude of self-confidence others will believe in you. Are you well "supplied" with the knowledge, the tools of your goal achievement? When you have made an honest, thorough self-inspection and know everything to be in order, "Highball!"

You Have the Line-Up

Once I have made a satisfactory air test, I will be told to "highball". The tracks and signals will be "lined-up" for my departure. I "have the line-up and can highball out of town."

Yet, in spite of all the preparation and inspections, highballs, and line-ups, the train will go nowhere unless I take the throttle in hand and made the first move.

The smell of worn metal, diesel fuel, dust and the Old Spice of my head brakeman mingle in the stuffy cab of the engine.

The radio, a static sound of activity, orders and comments shouted over the clang of engine bells, motors and other background noise, combines with the steady hum (sometimes roar) of the engine keeping cadence with my heart. My Headbrakeman perched on his seat to my left, looking out the window to the ground seemingly miles between us, somewhat hidden from view by the neck-high control console on my left. Three thousand horsepower in my left hand, a hand filled with the cold steel of the throttle.

All these things so familiar yet never have I sat in the Engineers seat without a feeling of sheer terror! Terror bred by the knowledge that one quarter of a million dollars worth of engine, from one to eleven thousand tons of freight and equipment and a minimum of four lives all depend on me.

Yet, when I bring the throttle out to "Run", I have made that first and hardest step and now we are on our way.

Milepost 4

Take that first positive step. All the wishes, plans and ingenious ideas are all of no use to you unless you act on them. Get that train rolling and keep it on the right track.

No Opposing on the Harbor

Delays and obstacles, unfortunately are occurrences every Engineer has learned to expect and as much as possible plan for (there is that word again, plan.)

Before the Extra Harbor train leaves the Los Angeles yard area, the control station will call and inform me of any other "opposing" trains on the "Harbor" district. These would be known obstacles and ones I can plan to meet. There are, however, other obstacles I may encounter, debris piled on the track by pranksters, children throwing rocks at the engine and any number of mechanical engine failures. These I must handle as they occur. I do not walk off the train and leave it.

September 1977, Topeka, Kansas is the home of the simulator training school for locomotive engineers of the Santa Fe railway. It is six weeks of intensive learning.

My first week I spent each day from 8:00 a.m. to 5:00 p.m. in Rules, Air and Train Handling and Mechanical Classes. From 5:00 to 5:45 p.m. was spent grabbing a box of Church's Fried Chicken and returning to my room at the nearby hotel. 5:45 to 6:15, I would run my bath water; a hot relaxing one, scour my face and hop in the tub. From approximately (depending on how soon the water got cold) 6:15 to 6:30 I took my bath, ate my chicken and studied my notes all simultaneously; which is great as long as you can remember which is the chicken and which is the soap. 6:30 to 6:40 I dressed for bed. 6:40 to 11:00 and often 1:00 a.m. I studied, memorized and usually developed chronic migraine headaches.

By Thursday of the first week, I became a mass of crying, hysterical and discouraged nerves.

Pistons and turbo-chargers? Ohms and Amps? Crankshafts and gear-ratios and me . . . the only one in class who mistook a "short closed bend" for a "short clothespin".

I was trying so hard and my goal was so near, but there was so much to learn. Oh . . . what if I didn't make it? A reservoir of tears filled a box of Kleenex.

With the Kleenex spent and my composure regained I placed a call to my parents' home where my two sons were staying. During the course of the conversation with my ten year-old, Suede Lee, he asked me how school was going. Oops, wrong question, another reservoir of tears for the Kleenex box.

His reaction to all this? "Now Mom, you're gonna' study and I'm gonna' pray. So how can you fail?"

I hung up that phone, plugged in the coffee pot and the following Monday passed all my tests.

Don't let obstacles stop your train. Remember, a rolling train is more powerful than one standing still.

Milepost 5

Determine to overcome all obstacles. You will have them, everyone does, but it's those who do not see them as obstacles but merely problems to be solved that are the successful people we admire.

"Tie up and Take the Power to the House"

"Santa Fe engine 8737 to Watson Yard, where would you like us to put the train?"

"Watson Yard to the 8737. Put your train in track three, tie-up and take your power to the house."

Notice that he didn't tell me to shut my engine down; only to tie-up, rest for awhile and take my engine to the 'house' where it can be refueled and readied for another trip.

I have reached the station at the end of the line, but that is not the last trip I'll take, not the last train I'll handle and Watson Yard not the last station on every line.

The dragon throws more than one Pearl of Potentiality.

Milepost 6

You've had a good run. You identified your goal. You studied and planned your route. You overcame obstacles and kept that train rolling on the right track.

So, "tie-up" and take your power to the house. Put your feet up and rest a bit, have a cup of coffee. Then check your railroad watch, slap that engineer's hat back on, and grab your grip, cause . . . "She'll be coming around the mountain. . . ."

Highballing up the right track . . .

AGAIN!

Grace Batts
14430 East Valley Blvd.
City of Industry, CA 91746
(213) 961-9481

GRACE BATTS

Grace Batts is . . . a dynamic, red-head dedicated to Sharing Opportunity with everyone she meets, born in Scotland, mother of 3 and proud grandmother of eight beautiful grandchildren. She married John Batts, a building contractor, who has been instrumental in helping her create Grace Unlimited.

Hollywood Make Up Artist, authority on Skin Care and women in general . . . Grace has an unending background in every phase of Cosmetics and is known as the "Original Traveling Sales Lady" and Woman's Equality in action.

Grace was a Sales Trainer for American National Life Insurance, a Representative for Irma Coleman Beauty Products, Coty's, Richard Hudnut Products and Helena Rubenstein. She entered the Direct Selling Field with Viviane Woodard Cosmetics as a Direct District Distributor and trained with Gordon Bau, President of the Society of Make Up Artists, head of Warner Brothers' Studio Make Up Department. While working with Mr. Bau, she learned many new techniques and secrets used on the stars and was instrumental in creating many make-up concepts for some of the stars.

Grace then joined Con-Stan Industries as a Vice President and became an international traveler, discovering many new methods and ingredients for beautiful, healthy skin care. She co-founded Concept Now Cosmetics and after seven years began her own Company, *Grace Unlimited, Incorporated.* Grace with her Enthusiasm creates new vistas of opportunity in the Direct Sales World.

> "Blaw yer 'pipes, and beat yer drum
> The best of life is yet to come!"
>
> FROM ANCIENT SCOTLAND

"Rooted within oneself is the source of all influence. Without effort or intent, by our inner attitude we move those of like spirit. To voice a feeling truthfully, to express a sentiment in clear action exerts a mysterious and far reaching influence."
TAO

"Hele On!" NOT TO WORRY! YOU MAKE YOUR DREAMS BIG ENOUGH

by Grace Batts

These words from my father motivated me all of my life, and I heard them loud and clear the day I bought and paid cash for my very first, big, white, fan-tailed Cadillac; installed a luxurious 18 by 30 swimming pool, and as I sat in my beautiful home on top of a hill, watching the lights go on in homes from Los Angeles to Pomona; or as I collected the rents from the apartments, my husband had built for me with my Party Plan money. Were my *dreams big enough?*

My Roots Began . . .

. . . in a tiny little seacoast village in Ayrshire, Scotland, in Robert Burn's country, where the ocean constantly lapped against the skirtboard of our wee cottage. One of seven children, I was third eldest, born to the most beautiful, loving parents one could ask for. My memories of that time were of a little cottage, filled with singing, much laughter, love and prayers, my father playing a melodeon or any musical instrument he picked up; my mother's beautiful voice singing the auld Scots' songs, a kettle hanging over the open fire, ready to make a cup of tea for whomever dropped in: and always Love, Gentleness and Kindness.

If We Love One Another God Dwells In Us!

Of course money-wise we were very poor, but we were *rich in love,* laughter, singing, and friends. With all of this, my parents wanted much more for their children; a chance to be Whatever We Dared To Be. At that time, Scotland had a highly prejudiced "Caste System". My father being a miner by trade meant we lived in a mining world. My brothers could only be miners, we girls would marry miners, our friends all miners, etc., and that is the way the system went.

My parents were determined to take us to America, the "Land of Opportunity." They saved every cent they could. My enterprising mother, bless her heart, became a "Hawker," (one who buys clothes from the more fortunate, in turn selling them to the poor), and was successful enough. So that the big day of our lives came; our departure time. I remember how we waved goodbye to our remaining family with tears streaming down our faces, and my precious little 4'11" granny, my darling grandfather, whom we called Da, standing there growing smaller and smaller, as we pulled out to sea. We were never to see them again. My last sad rememberance of them was with their arms around each other, a beautiful couple. Bless their dear hearts!

We were soon heading for our new lives in America, the land where "money grows on trees, and the streets were paved with solid gold. Where Opportunity Abounded for everyone and people were equal and free." We didn't then know that we would have two very hard years to survive in Canada before being allowed to enter into this wonderful country of America. It took 2½ years for our quota number to come up and we were ready.

It was the month of August when the Magic Day arrived. We scrambled aboard the Ferry boat from Windsor, Ontario, Canada across the river to Detroit, Michigan, U.S.A., landing at beautiful Belle Isle Park, (without a red cent left to our names). Most people would have been panic-stricken but my father very calmly warned us to mind our mother and be good. He showed us a tall, clean, white drinking fountain (we had never seen one before). He said we could have *all* the drinking water we wanted. Well, we'd never had all we wanted of any*"thing"* in our lives before, so we really gave that fountain one big workout. He said he'd return for us before dark, and true to his word he returned with enough money to rent a room for the night in a nearby rooming house; plus, he had purchased a loaf of bread, a quart of milk, and a few ham slices and, of course, tea for Mother. He had knocked on doors offering to wash windows at 2¢ a window and found people eager to hire him. He did this every day until we could afford to rent an upper flat by the week. Then Dad finally got a full-time job with the Ford Motor Company and we began to eat two, or sometimes even three, meals a day. We became settled in school and everything was going well. "Life was Beautiful." We were happy - we were loved and learning.

Then one morning we awoke to full scale tragedy. The Wall Street collapse of 1929; no jobs, etc. . . . As a family we immediately began to pull together and took whatever jobs we could get. We sold newspapers, shoveled snow, baby sat, cut grass, any job at all, big or small. My parents were honest, proud Scots, who never considered welfare, or borrowing money. We'd 'make out' on our own somehow, and we did. I can never remember having our electric and gas on at the same time. My mother had to cook on an old kerosene stove someone gave us. What a dirty mess.

But we hung together, and always had the love, music, singing and the comfort of being in America "the Land of Opportunity."

When I was in the eighth grade I read an ad for "help wanted" in the Cosmetics Department at the J. L. Hudson Company. I put my long hair up, àla Kay Frances (a big star of that time), and created what I then thought was a very sophisticated look. I spent hours on my knees before my heavenly Father, then took off to apply for the job at 35¢ an hour. WOW! That 35¢ bought a loaf of bread, a stick of butter and a dozen eggs. *"I got the job."* Immediately I fell in love with the world of cosmetics, selling, and the benefits they brought me. This is the time in my life *when I caught my first* "Pearl of Potentiality."

Nothing was too hard, no job too small. I was willing, eager to learn, and a diligent worker. I was an apt pupil with a very hungry mind, and not too proud to question everyone. Even on my lunch breaks instead of eating, I prowled the store to find out in which department was the greatest opportunity for making money. I discovered a little, 5'2" blond lady, who swirled into the store at 10 A.M. in her little fox cape and left at 4 P.M., while we cleaned and prepared her counter and work area.

She did "open demonstrations," (applying makeup to her own face) while talking and she earned *$100.00* per week, with an additional 3% on everything she sold. I immediately began a campaign through the buyer to allow me to "cashier" for that lady. I would get an additional 1% on everything sold from that booth. I began to visualize myself as her cashier and six weeks later . . . I was her Cashier! Man! I really learned to love percentages. Instead of earning $15.00 a week, I now made a whopping $20.00 a week. I began to learn all I could about cosmetics and their presentation; every word of her spiel, every gesture, every selling phrase. She was such a ham. (Now I know why I'm a ham today.) When I felt I knew everything by rote, I prayed and visualized myself sitting behind that counter demonstrating and selling. (I have a wonderful Partner, one who not only hears, but answers my prayers as well.) The demonstrator called in. She was too ill to come to work . . . "Thank You Heavenly Partner!" The Buyer told me to shut down the counter, as without a demonstrator—there would be few sales. I begged him to "Please Give Me the Opportunity of trying my skills as a demonstrator!" He said, "No." I was too little, only weighing 86 lbs. and not quite 5 foot at the time. I promised him if he would give Me the Opportunity, I would double the volume. "Please just give me a chance."

I visualized my catching that opportunity with all my might, and finally the Buyer said "O.K.!" He gave me an assistant, a darling Polish girl, whom I knew was a real sales closer. She was a perfect teammate and encouraged me 100%. I was almost invisible behind the counter, so I sent a stock boy to bring me a wooden soap box to stand on and raise me up a foot or so.

Now I was ready; but gosh, no one stopped at my counter. *I was determined* to do the job. Using my imagination, I went to one of the cosmetic counters and bought an old, dried up, harsh colored rouge. Then on to the toiletries department, where I borrowed their most beautiful gold inlaid and pure ivory hand mirror; then up on my soap box spreading this horrible rouge all over my face, holding up this gorgeous mirror and talking aloud to myself. A dear little old lady stopped at my counter, (she must have thought I was out of my mind.) "Child, what are you doing?" I grabbed that little lady and told her to stand there and I would show her. I took the cleansing cream and began to demonstrate how well it cleaned off that awful red guck. I knew full well all I needed was one person to stop and watch, and very quickly a crowd would gather. Once we began that demonstration our sales did not stop all day long. At 5:40 P.M. (store closed at 5:30 in those days) we were still selling to all those wonderful people. At the close of that day we had reached our goal and doubled the volume, just as I had promised the buyer. *Determine in Your Mind What You Really Want . . .* then *Visualize it,* and *"Do It."* It will work for you, it worked for me! Don't say "I will try." *"Try"* is merely the back door to failure.

The next day the demonstrator came in and gave me the job permanently. Incidentally she was the owner of the company. Irma Coleman, wherever you are, I owe you a lot. You are the beautiful dragon who threw me the first "Pearl of Potentiality" and I am eternally grateful. Thank you for your faith in me.

Original Traveling Sales Lady

Irma told me she would teach me how to travel and open up other stores and train women to do what I did. True to her word, in 12 weeks I became the "Original Traveling Sales Lady," for Irma Coleman Cosmetics. In those days your whole family went to the airport with tears in their eyes to say good-bye because you were going on a long plane trip, and they might never see you again. I was traveling a whole 280 miles from Detroit to Cleveland —Cincinnatti, Ohio, and even as far away as St. Louis, Missouri which was all of 500 miles from home. I discovered I loved to travel, to train new people and most of all to teach others; however my greatest discovery was I loved people and was thrilled to be part of their growth. I got hooked on seeing people catch their own "Pearl of Potentiality."

At Christmas I met the love of my life, Jack Batts, and we were married. We have been blessed with many happy years together.

For 13 years I traveled with cosmetics, and had by this time been with many major companies and enjoyed each experience, tremendous growth and know-how.

I came home from Gimbels in Milwaukee, Wisconsin, to learn that *Jack* and I were to *suddenly* become parents of 3 children. A baby boy 5 months old, a girl 17 months, and a boy 2½ years. What beautiful children they were. We had been hoping for children and had applied for adoption 10 years earlier. Then a friend who worked for the Baptist children's home told us of three beautiful orphans who needed parents. Our hearts melted! Today they are all grown and successful, and have given us eight beloved grandchildren.

In one day I went from being a glamorous traveling career girl to being a mother. (Being a career girl was much easier.)

The children's health was under par, sicknesses caused from malnutrition and just plain neglect. It was our desire to see them normal, happy, healthy children. Jack and I had bought some property a few years earlier in El Monte, California. Now we decided to leave cold, snowy Michigan and bring our children to this healthy, warm climate. We moved to California and built a lovely home for them. I began to study and research good nutrition and natural foods, my goal being to make "our three" as healthy and sturdy as possible. What beautiful children, and what a change in our lifestyle but we loved our "wee" three and the daily blessings they brought into our lives, we thanked God each day for bringing them to us. . . .

String of Pearls

We soon ran out of money and had a need to earn extra dollars. My precious sister introduced me to a Food Supplement that worked wonders for all of us. As we were so into nutrition, it was a natural for us to tell others about this product and we found it so easy to sell. Jack and I very quickly became managers for ViSan Food Supplement, where we met many wonderful people, one of whom was the well known Dr. Gordon K. Woodard. He owned many pharmaceutical houses and had created "ViSan Food Supplement Co." to sell his products with a fair and honest marketing plan.

I had also started working with make-up again, and met Gordon Bau, who was head make-up man at Warner Brothers, and President of the Society of Make-up Artists. He began to teach me make-up techniques. I quickly became his eye brow expert and had the pleasure of working with stars from television and motion pictures. Along with this, I'd taken a job with American National Life Insurance out of Monterey Park, and was their first Woman Sales Trainer. I worked, carrying a "debit" (debit is a weekly insurance plan) and this now became one of the most interesting times in my life. I also did part time Sales Training for Great Books of the Western World in Los Angeles. It was interesting to train men in selling. Up to this time, my only experience had been with women.

The Dragon Returns!

I was actually working with four businesses at the same time! In order to make the money I needed I had to be away from my children and I was missing all the cute things children say and do. Then another Pearl came my way! Dr. Woodard, the ViSan President, decided he would put together a new, exciting and prestigious cosmetic company, "Viviane Woodard Cosmetics." He would use the Party Plan world of direct selling to introduce his exciting new theory of holding moisture into the skin. I was thrilled to be offered this opportunity and be able to work with my first love, cosmetics. I concentrated on only Viviane Woodard and quickly gathered together a sales group. I was enthusiastic with the concept of the cosmetics. I soon opened my own office in Rosemead, California and became one of the top National Distributing Directors for Viviane Woodard. I loved it! My enthusiasm lit fires in the people I worked with as I tossed pearls of opportunity to them. I was now working for myself, my own boss, and most of all *free* to spend all the time I wanted with my children. Most exciting of all, I had learned how to book a show, recruit people to work with me, and run an organization. I earned *more money* than I formerly had with any other company, growing my own "party plan money tree." I loved the freedom to plan my own time. I stayed with Viviane Woodard for years until I met an exciting man, Mulford Nobbs, the founder of Con Stan Industries. He had another party plan. This man gave me even more latitude with freedom in building and working with people around the world. Soon I was traveling in every state of the union, in every town and in many foreign countries. *I learned that all people are beautiful, warm, human beings.* I loved working with them as individuals and helping them to catch sight of their own pearls of potentiality. I was even sent back to Scotland, the land of my birth, which was a thrilling emotional bonus. There "Nobby" (Mulford Nobbs) gave me the privilege of taking my English, Irish, Scottish cousins by the hand, and introducing them to Party Plan, earning and learning how to catch their own "Pearls of Potentiality." I met women everywhere and had the privilege of showing them how to find their own personal and financial freedom. He gave me the opportunity to meet and find friends around the world. I felt a love in my heart toward all people.

Another Opportunity

Next, I co-founded "Concept Now Cosmetics" in partnership with Rita Berro Gross, and again loved working with many wonderful people who put forth much effort. We built a fantastic company. I'm grateful to say this company has now become a major force in the Direct Selling Field. In every venture in which we participate and contribute in life we experience and grow. Then we are ready to catch the next opportunity and challenge.

It is Now Time to Step Out in Faith . . .

. . . with the loyal support of many wonderful people, friends, family (my precious sisters) and most of all my darling husband, on March 4, 1979, we formed a new corporation and started our own cosmetic company, *Grace Unlimited, Incorporated* (named for me, and my life in America). We have an exciting concept of Rose Hip (vitamin C) skin care. Although we are new, we are already established in Japan, Canada, Hawaii and many states in

America. The land of opportunity fulfilled my parents' dreams. They are overjoyed that we came to this great land. They are proud of our hard work, industry and faith.

God is blessing us mightily. "Whatever we put into the lives of others, comes back into our own *tenfold*".

I am the luckiest woman in the world and I have learned in my varied career that the love I receive into my own life and the friendships I have formed, are my most precious possession, plus the love of God and country. I firmly believe that each of us can catch our "Pearl of Potentiality". Opportunity comes flying to us Time after Time. Often many of us reject it for the so-called "Security" of a 40-hour week. We allow ourselves to fall into a big rut, and what is a rut? Nothing but a "Grave with the Ends Kicked Out."

Security is taking charge of your own life, and taking advantage of every opportunity offered. Dare to take the risk and catch every pearl! So what if you should fail? "Hele On" as our Hawaiian sales people call to us. "Get up and go on again!" Hallelujah! You are one step closer to Success. There is no sweeter taste on earth than that of achievement and personal financial independence. As my Scottish ancestors said "Proud members of our clan, will bow down before no man!"

May the Lord Bless you Real Good, and you keep looking up!

Connie Yambert
2968 San Pasqual Street
Pasadena, CA 91107
(213) 681-4944

CONNIE YAMBERT

When Connie Yambert first enrolled in the Mullin/Dean Public Speaking Training Program she was the only woman in the class, the others were top level business and professional men. She realized in order to achieve any success in the business world that her pearl of great price for both business and social success would be in public speaking. Today she is the sole owner of Mullin/Dean Executive Speaking Training Program.

There are some who might say, she slept her way to the top, for indeed she was sleeping with her instructor, (husband) the late Ralph Yambert.

She is a much sought after speaker on the subjects of: Public Speaking, Growth and Achievement, Selling, Closing the Communication Gap, How to Conduct a Meeting, How to Tell Humorous Stories, Assertiveness, Growth Through Adversity, Anger Prevention, Creative Widowhood, Social and Business Etiquette.

Connie has been billed on television as the 'Merry Widow' because of her positive and constructive attitude toward an almost predictable human condition.

Connie trains business and professional people in public speaking and personal development. She is listed in Who's Who of The American Society of Training and Development, Director of Los Angeles Speakers Club, member of Women in Business, both Pasadena and Los Angeles Chamber of Commerce, and National Speakers Association. Connie conducts seminars nationally for business organizations and other interested groups.

Connie has three grown children, a daughter Whitney in San Francisco, another Sloane, in college and a son Bill in the Air Force.

5

For one word a person is often deemed to be wise, and for one word foolish. We should be careful what we say.
CONFUCIUS

MEND THY SPEECH, LEST IT MAR THY FORTUNE

by Connie Dean Yambert

There were times I bemoaned the fact that I had to pay off many of my late husband's debts, but that stopped one day in Houston, Texas. I was doing a training class for Allied Chemical Corporation, the corporate attorney was very impressed with our methods of teaching Executive Speaking and asked me how I learned these methods. I told him my late husband taught me and his reply was a resounding "Wow! What a legacy he left you."

I was training top level executives of one of the largest corporations in the world—all of whom were successful in their chosen field—and all of whom recognized the need for more effective verbal communications.

Conversely, when I was co-chairing an event and had to engage a speaker, my co-chairperson suggested a very prominent business man and I asked her if he were "a good speaker?" Her reply was "Of course, look at the position he holds." If the two went together I would not be in business. People are educated to be lawyers, accountants, engineers, physicians and dentists and other professions and are very good at their particular area of expertise—it simply does not follow that they are effective speakers unless they've been trained to be.

Now A Flashback

The first time I walked into his office for a job interview —I was struck by his incredibly good looks, he was six feet tall but stood like a giant, his soft blue eyes will never be forgotten for he mesmerized me with direct eye contact. He had a most engaging smile. I didn't know whether he was going to hire me or not but I was already sold on him. You know the old proverbial story, "She was gorgeous until she opened her mouth." It didn't apply here because when he opened his mouth I was even more impressed. His tones were perfectly placed and his diction was impeccable. It was undeniable that nothing could shake his self-confidence.

Does this sound like the beginning of a love story—no, it was just a working relationship which did develop into a love story five and one-half years later and a fully blessed marriage to Ralph Yambert two years after that. Now we'll flash back even further . . .

In the Beginning

My career beginnings were in New York City which is where I was born and educated. After two years of college I decided to loaf one summer when a classmate, Seena Donlan, called and said she was working in a Madison Avenue Ad Agency for the summer and urged me to apply for a position which was available in the Media Department. If it were anyplace but an ad agency, I would have continued my vacation but advertising always fascinated me. In those days it was safe to ride on the subway—I arrived, was interviewed and accepted as the assistant to the Media Director. Instantly I had a super role-model. The Media Director was my age and was doing all the media buying for many national accounts. She was referred to as "girl genius." I loved my job—even more than school, I found my career choice, and it didn't require a college degree so I left school to enter the business world. After three years in the Media Department of this rather large agency I wanted to diversify, so I went on to a medium sized ad agency and worked at various times as traffic manager, public relations director, account executive and media director. It was a glamour field and even before it was fashionable I was totally career oriented —my life was working! I had daily contact with many famous T.V. personalities.

California Here I Come

At that point I had traveled up and down the east coast but hadn't ventured west of the Poconos when a girlfriend, Jean Davis, suggested we go to California (eleven hours by air). My reply was "No way, I have everything I want right here in the world's most exciting city." Famous last words! Over the protests of my boss and lots of wonderful bribes, for instance, "I'll air-condition your office." (In those days not too many offices were air-conditioned.) The substantial raise was inviting but alas! I decided to embark on the adventure on a "six months leave of absence." The result was I arrived in Los Angeles and Jean didn't come until six years later—just for a visit.

Alone—But Not For Long

Here I was in my early twenties, had always been very protected by an adoring father and a large close-knit family, alone and 3,000 miles away from home. The young man in the next apartment was an electrical engineer, Bill Otto, who had just returned from three years in Saudi Arabia. Four months later we were married and I settled down to the role of housewife and mother. (That was what we were supposed to do, wasn't it?) The career fell by the wayside. I guess I took this very seriously because in the first six years of marriage we had four children. Then tragedy struck, my three year old son, Schuyler, passed away. It was a devastating experience. My values did a 180 degree turn from the material to the spiritual. We had a lovely house in the San Rafael area of Pasadena, a second home in Palm Springs, a luxury automobile in the garage, a swimming pool in the backyard, a full time housekeeper, my husband was devoted and loyal—and I was miserable!! I adored my children—but twenty four hours a day? My son, Bill, was hyperactive. Mothers of hyperactive children—take heart, they do outgrow it. I never considered giving him any medication, it was rough on both of us—but we hung in there. Today he is twenty three years old, in the U.S. Air Force stationed in San Bernardino, and I look forward to him coming home every weekend. Today he is one of the greatest delights of my life. My reward for the patience and love I expressed to him when I thought I really wanted to kill him. Extreme language? Ask any mother who has had an H-A child.

From Housewife to Businesswoman

With the pressure of dealing with little Bill and the other children, a wonderful but non-communicative husband, my total detachment from the outside world made me feel like a zombie residing in a mausoleum rather than a lovely home in Pasadena.

About this time, the Women's Lib Movement was really coming into being and when I came home one day and announced to my husband that I had accepted a job (after being a housewife for twelve years) I had to peel him off the ceiling. After all, I was a wife, I was a mother, he could afford to support me and buy me diamonds and furs— Good Lord, is that all there is? He threatened to divorce me—"If I were going to work, why did I need him?" Now we're back to the work interview I started with at the beginning of the chapter. I was hired as the account executive on the American Savings and Loan Account at the Ralph Yambert Organization. Later when the account moved on to another agency, Mr. Yambert kept me on as Media Director. My husband did not divorce me—as a matter of fact, I could not have continued in this demanding job without his cooperation and support which he gave lovingly.

After seventeen years of marriage to Bill Otto we were divorced. Bill was a wonderful, devoted husband and father. Temperamentally we were totally unsuited to each other.

A Total Love Affair—The Second Time Around

Seven years after my job interview I married this handsome, exciting man I described earlier. We all want that wonderful, perfect, compatible and mutual love relationship—few find it—I was one of the fortunate ones. Mary Baker Eddy, Founder of Christian Science, said "Marriage is often a convenience, sometimes pleasant, *only occasionally a love affair*—and it sometimes presents the most wretched condition of human existence."

He was indeed a very exciting man. He, the children and I moved to a large, beautiful home in Newport Beach. His ad agency occupied offices across from the Orange County Airport which made it very convenient to walk to the airport, board his private plane and take off to perhaps Palm Springs, Las Vegas, Bakersfield for dinner. I took the Aircraft Owners' and Pilots' Association pinch hitters flying course which I highly recommend to the companion of any private pilot. Ralph was a member of the Wilshire Country Club—I took golf lessons and we played together on weekends. We laughed together, played together, loved together and worked together—it was sheer joy.

Tragedy Revisited

After just a few years of complete ecstasy my world collapsed around me. Ralph became terminally ill, he had absolutely no medical or hospital coverage—the high cost of health care wiped all of "the good life" away —BANKRUPTCY! It was necessary to shut the doors on our thriving little agency in Newport and move to Pasadena to a less affluent way of life. Ralph then returned to and bought back a business he had many years ago—a training program in Public Speaking and Personal Development.

A New Career

Now Connie Dean Yambert was unwittingly being prepared for a second career in mid-life. I was terrified when Ralph suggested I participate as a student in his public speaking course. I resisted, I protested, "One public speaker in the family is enough"—and I found out that your husband's talents do not rub off on you. The beguiling factor was "Honey, we can be together." In the beginning I thought I'd be so overcome with fear that I'd probably faint. When I gave the first six talks I couldn't see faces in the audience, it was just one great mass. I suffered, I agonized, and he encouraged. One hundred and seventy five talks later, *yes 175,* he urged me to start teaching the classes. I loved it! He and I taught classes together in Los Angeles, Newport Beach, San Fernando Valley and Pasadena. I didn't know what God was preparing me for at that time, but Ralph passed away March 1, 1974, I was able to carry on as head of Mullin/Dean and Associates. It was not easy. Not only was my love affair over but his illness left us deeply in debt. I faced the biggest difficulty in my life at a stage where I presumed life would be a total joy with the children grown and on their own. In addition to the regular classes I started doing special classes for top level executives in corporations nation-wide.

There is nothing that gives you quite so much dignity as what you can do for yourself. It's the old story of "If you give a man a fish you feed him for a day—but if you teach him how to fish, you feed him for a lifetime." It made me realize that some other widows I knew who were well provided for financially were 'wallowing' around either at home or in the hospital in self-pity. I had time for neither illness nor self-pity.

Through my business contacts I have met some dynamite men and women, I have joined some very worthwhile organizations including National Speakers Association. But most of all I am performing a very useful and badly needed function. I will be eternally grateful to my darling husband for his persistence in training me in Public Speaking.

Who Are Our Clients?

According to the Book of Lists speaking before a group is the number one worst human fear. I can identify with that—but I also know it can be healed in every individual who has the desire to eliminate that fear. Just as I was taught I am teaching others.

These are actual case histories:

1. A gentleman, who is president of a large corporation whose name you would recognize, confided to me when he was investigating our training that he'd go into the bathroom and throw up everytime he had to speak before a group. The first time it happened was in his college Public Speaking class and he continued the pattern for years before taking our training. He still gets butterflies, but at least they're flying in formation and he no longer gets sick!

2. A professional man who had so much anxiety before a very important talk he had to give that his vocal cords constricted and when he got up to speak no sound came out! He was led from the room with a gentleman patting him on the arm saying, "It's all right, Mr. X, we're all your friends."

3. The engineer who was a borderline alcoholic, had to give a talk representing his company. He did so poorly, misrepresented his company in his confusion and lack of organization, he was fired from his job, was pushed over the brink into alcoholism, his wife divorced him—and only then did he call us!

4. The business woman who walked off stage when she couldn't command the attention of the audience, became hostile, screamed at her audience that it was "their fault" and left in tears. It reduced the stature of a very capable business woman.

These are some of the people who come to us and there are many similar cases. There are also those who have minimal or practically no fear of standing before a group but agonize over "gathering and preparing" their material. Still others who do not know the proper way to organize their material, or they are unaware of the rules of poise in speaking, or how to paint vivid word pictures, tell humorous stories or chair a meeting, use a microphone or how to get adequate volume, range, tone, inflection and voice placement for the maximum effectiveness. What about facial animation or physical action, eye contact, how to eliminate the "ahs" "ums" and "and ahs." How to avoid distracting mannerisms like twisting a ring, adjusting eye glasses, leaning on the lectern, fingering notes, reading (God forbid). Clete Roberts once said "Listening to a 'read speech' is an invitation to boredom!"

I hope I've been able to show here that there is a great deal more to effective speaking than merely "knowing your subject" or being "enthusiastic." Is an effective speaker ever "just born that way?" Yes, about as often as a child prodigy is "just born that way"—and can play Chopin at the age of three.

It has come to my attention that some professionally trained speakers do not admit that they've had training. It has something to do with an "ego" problem. More and more they are "coming out of the closet."

Drab Black and White or Living Color

Sometime ago a very well-trained public speaker was asked to share the program at a professional society meeting with another speaker, an actor turned business man. He was very self-confident explaining to our student that his acting training had provided him with a great deal of stage presence. She was asked to give her talk first. She did such a dynamite job that the former actor was so intimidated he was unable to follow her. True story. To illustrate, if you had never seen a television set in your life and a friend arrives with this marvelous new invention, a twelve inch black and white TV set, imagine walking, talking pictures in your own home. Super! But then another friend brings you a thirty inch solid state color set, which would you watch? Now reverse it, you're presented with the color set first—wouldn't our actor friend be a twelve inch black and white.

Let's Talk About You

So much for me, so much for them—now let's talk about YOU. If you are reading this book, you are probably on your quest for your "Pearl of Potentiality"—one of the quickest ways to get there from here is through Public Speaking. It will enhance your opportunities for both business and social success.

The fact is that in business all speaking is "Public Speaking." Ninety percent of the people who come to us do not necessarily come to be public speakers. They are business and professional people who want to improve their communication skills. The people you come in contact with everyday in business don't usually stick around long enough to discover what a great sincere, loving person you are. They are usually around long enough to judge us by the way we look and the way we speak.

How To Organize The Way You Speak

The purpose of the introduction: To gain audience attention. There are six proven methods:

1. Illustration or word picture
2. Humorous story (*only* if it relates to your subject.)
3. Quotations
4. Verse of poetry
5. Series of three or more questions
6. Startling statement

The purpose of the conclusion: To wrap up your message in a neat little package and give it to the audience to take away with them. There are six proven methods. The first four are the same as above. A word of caution, if your talk is a serious one do not conclude with a humorous story. Do not conclude with questions—they require answers. A startling statement needs to be qualified, so, try.

5. A summary
6. An appeal or an urge

Regarding the body and other bits of information:

1. Never announce your subject.
2. Never start with an apology
3. Stick to the subject.
4. Follow a logical sequence.
5. Use the "You" attitude
6. Entertain as well as Instruct

Poise

Perhaps you have not realized that Public "speaking" is visual as well as auditory and you must look as well as sound like a speaker. If you were having a photograph taken you would be very conscious of your appearance —standing before a group is much the same as being before a camera. Each member of the audience is "recording" your appearance as well as your speaking. Anything you do to indicate a lack of poise is detracting from your message—even so much as picking up a paper clip.

One of the first rules of poise is stand with your feet together—never apart which tends to make your stomach jut out and shoulders round. Distribute weight evenly on both feet, shoulders erect. Maintain eye contact with your entire audience—*not* just a single person. Look at the members of your audience on the left side, then on the right, in front and in back. If direct eye contact makes you uncomfortable, look at their chins, forehead or ears. They will never know you're not looking directly at them. What do you do with your hands until you're very comfortable and will then be gesturing naturally, simply fold them in front of you or in back of you.

A Speaker is an Artist With Words

You have perhaps never realized that a speaker is something of an artist. The usual conception of an artist is a person who creates a picture upon canvas or paper. To create this picture he uses paint, pencil, crayon, or pen and ink. A speaker, on the other hand, is an artist who creates pictures with words. His pictures should be just as vivid and can be every bit as beautiful as those originated by a portrait painter or an illustrator.

A prime psychological fact is that the human mind is so constituted as to better receive and retain pictures than any other medium. A word, as such, has no memory value. If it is pictured vividly, however, your mind will retain it for a long period. As proof of this fact, you can no doubt immediately call to mind the happiest experience you have ever had. You can picture every detail of a scene which has etched itself upon your consciousness. Now try to remember a page from a book on accounting that you have read. Impossible, isn't it?

By applying this same fact to a talk you will see that if you inject only facts and figures into your subject your audience will be unable to remember them for long. They'll be entirely disinterested in them as well. On the other hand, if you take the same facts and picture them vividly, you not only put over an interesting message, but your listeners will carry your thoughts away with them.

The first rule of speaking, then, is illustrate! Paint mental pictures of every fact you wish to emphasize.

Learn to Speak in Pictures

Illustrating as you talk is really just as easy as it sounds. You can tell an interesting incident much more easily than you can state a series of facts.

An actual illustration is accomplished by "setting the stage" with time, place and characters and then telling the "story."

All talks should be built around actual illustrations. While it is true that all illustrations used cannot be expected to be actual, the main ones in any talk should be. Sometimes a little imagination can be used to transform an illustration that didn't actually occur into one that seems to have occurred. Your picture will not be weakened by the omission of true names. But it will be considerably strengthened if it is told as an actual happening.

Sources of Illustrations

An open mind, a seeing eye, an alert ear, will provide a steady flow of illustrations for the speaker. You walk to work. You see an incident. It can be transformed into a vivid mental picture for a talk. Or, you read a book. A situation in the book is used for another talk. A magazine article provides other pictures.

You will soon learn, as you develop your speaking ability, that your thinking ability improves as well. Recently a student remarked, "I never realized how much I was missing until I started this training. I even find myself thinking differently now. I retain what I read. I have started a scrap book. Whenever something appeals to me, into that scrap book it goes. I find I now have a steadily mounting fund of information which provides unlimited material for my talks."

You'll never forget the thrill that comes with the realization that training in Public Speaking is equipping you to muster your thoughts along a more orderly pattern. Your daily life will become a richer fount of experiences. Your reading will serve the double purpose of providing information and of stimulating thought.

The suggestion of keeping a scrapbook for the permanent filing of illustrations that appeal to you is a good one. Being sure that you are reading the correct material is another suggestion equally as good. Newspapers are excellent reading and should not be dispensed with. But too many people confine their reading to newspapers, a trade magazine or two, and perhaps a fiction magazine. Books chosen are, unfortunately, usually read for enjoyment only.

In addition to your favorite daily newspaper, *Time* magazine and *Reader's Digest* are two publications that should be read from cover to cover by every speaker. Other magazines such as 'U.S. News', 'Quote', 'Fortune', 'People', are also good, as are others. Base your reading habits upon the quality of the publications you choose. Read good books also. Non-fiction is better as a stimulant to your own thought than fiction. This isn't to be construed as meaning that all fiction is bad or that no fiction is good. It is merely an observation of a busy person who finds his own time so limited that his reading must be chosen with extreme care.

When you read, however, *retain*. It is a good idea to drop your magazine or book into your lap occasionally and just think over what you have read.

The ability to speak "in pictures" implies the ability to think "in pictures." Try to cultivate your pictorial sense by analyzing the illustrations in your daily reading. Note how many activities of your daily life can be related in illustrative form rather than in a factual manner. Some constructive thought along this line will add zest not only to your speaking but also to your writing and conversation.

For the purpose of this chapter I've included limited information on the skills of effective speaking. For more comprehensive material I'd be delighted to discuss it with anyone who wishes to contact me. To write it would fill a very thick book.

In Closing

Some points I'd like to stress are:

1. Don't hesitate to make a career change at any age. It's depressing to think of going through your entire life doing something you don't enjoy for the sake of "security." The most secure people in the world are in prison. They are provided with a place to live, food to eat, medical and dental care, etc. etc. Break out of your self-imposed prison and capture your Pearl of Potentiality.

2. Prepare. Remember Opportunity always comes to those who are prepared. One of the first ways to prepare is through professional public speaking training.

3. Experience it for yourself. Henry Ford said, "Whether you believe you can do a thing or not, you're right."

Press On!

Lois Jacobini
1211 Connecticut Ave. #403
Washington, D.C. 20036
(202) 466-3136

LOIS JACOBINI

Lois Jacobini is a nationally known analyst and consultant in the energy field. Her company, Washington Experts, Ltd., does specialized research and consulting with some of the nation's largest corporations and energy companies on such critical issues as U.S. energy policy.

Ms. Jacobini is much in demand as a public speaker, not only in the areas of her technical expertise, but to general audiences on motivational topics. With her spontaneity and enthusiasm, she is able to energize and inspire an audience with the story of her own success and her secrets for living a happy and fulfilled life.

"Space flights are merely an escape of flying away from oneself. It is easier to go to the moon than it is to penetrate one's own being."
JUNG

T-O-O-D-L-E-S

by Lois Jacobini

I ascribe much of my career success and personal happiness to a key phrase in my life—TOODLES!!! The Dictionary of American Slang defines toodles as a flip way of saying "goodbye." But as you will see, to me toodles means *change,* and it has been through a constant process of change that I have been able to prosper professionally and to find personal happiness.

I am the President and sole owner of Washington Experts, Ltd., a research and consulting firm specializing in energy matters. My company is less than four years old but we have been able to assemble a client list which includes many of the nation's largest corporations, many oil companies, major industry trade associations, and some of the most prestigious Washington, New York and

Houston law firms because we are able to provide an almost unique research and analysis service. My staff and I are able to supply the information and political intelligence vital to businesses dealing with the government and we do it with a speed and accuracy which has brought these clients to us and made them only too happy to pay our fees.

Several weeks ago I was having a business dinner at Joe & Mo's, one of Washington's top restaurants, with a client; a senior officer of a major oil company. He had requested the meeting and had flown in from Houston to ask my advice on how his company should respond to a part of President Carter's proposed new energy plan that could have a multi-million dollar effect on his company.

During the course of the dinner the executive started talking about a vacation he was planning for the holiday season and for some reason this got me to thinking of Christmas eight years ago and my introduction to Washington. I doubt that few have ever come to the nation's capital quite as scared or in quite as humble a situation.

For me it began in October, 1971 with a wrenching separation from all my friends, my home, comfortable and familiar surroundings and a broken marriage. I was leaving a casual life with little focus or intellectual challenge: a life in which I had been drifting along. I had been married at age 18 and had my son Billy at age 19 and now my marriage was over. It was time to go. I now would have to swallow my pride and ask for help from my family in Washington, a totally new environment for me. I knew the break needed my total commitment.

As we left Texas my four and a half year old son, bewildered at the turn of events, looked up at me and said, "Mom, if you still loved my dad I would still have a daddy." What seemed to be the last thread holding me together snapped, with my heart. Yet several hours later when I greeted my family at the Washington airport I had mastered a sparkle in my voice and a big smile. This confused them. They thought I would be upset and crying and had expected to be meeting an emotional wreck. How could I have changed my mood just during that short plane ride. I'll let you in on my secret. On the plane I retrieved from my childhood sunday school days what for me was the perfect inspiration. It was the biblical story about Lot and his wife. As we are told in Genesis, the Lord was about to destroy the evil cities of Sodom and Gomorra. Lot was the only good man in the region and the Lord decided to spare him and his family. On the morning of the destruction, an angel appeared to Lot and told him, "Take your wife and two daughters and flee for your life . . . do not look behind you." Lot and his daughters did as the angel instructed but Lot's wife did not. She looked back even as Lot continued to move forward and, as you will remember, she was turned into a pillar of salt.

I realized that although I had no idea what direction my life would take from this point on, I would have to always look ahead and continue to move forward. I knew as the lyrics of a popular song say, people lose tomorrow by looking back at yesterday. Thus I could put on a brave smile when I stepped off that plane to begin my new life in Washington.

So it was toodles Texas . . . hello Washington.

The Christmas Tree

My first job in Washington was a far cry from my current role of president of Washington Experts.

The first job opportunity came when I had applied to work in the office of a temporary staffing agency. Since I had developed no professional skills and had no formal higher education, I decided that working with people would be the most suitable for my primary attribute— enjoying people and communicating easily. Then the agency gave me my first assigment. They were responsible for filling a large chain of D.C. drug stores with Santas' helpers and were desperate for one more helper. I agreed to fill in for a couple of days, hoping that the manager of the temporary agency would appreciate my courage and willingness to help.

Just across the street from the Justice Department building stood a little drug store and in the front window was a Christmas Tree. Under it were Christmas toys, jumping loops, little puppies barking and wagging their tails, and monkeys clanging their cymbals. As you entered the door, there I was winding up all of the toys in my tiny red Santa costume with a great big smile on my face greeting the customers.

After a couple of days of playing Santa's helper, the agency asked me to help out in their office. I worked in the office for two weeks and was beginning to feel confident that I would land this job on a permanent basis. Unfortunately at the end of the second week the manager of the office clearly made me aware that he was desirous of my body. I explained to him that all I wanted was an opportunity to work hard and provide for my family and that I was not interested in him at all. I didn't get the job.

Although I did not get that job on a permanent basis, the Santa's helper job opened new avenues for me. The experience told me something about myself that I needed to know in order to continue my quest to find a real job. I discovered that although my skills were limited, I was competent and I now had gained confidence in myself. But how else would I have known except by doing it. Taking Action!

So it was toodles temporary . . . hello permanent.

Our Breakfast Club

My life was in forward motion. I landed a job as a bureaucrat working for the Postal Service's Finance Division. It was a light clerical job (very light). But it paid enough to allow me to rent a small basement apartment, and I rejoiced in achieving a measure of independence.

At this point I learned one of the great lessons of my life: *there is opportunity at every intersection if you stay in motion.* And in my case that included a government cafeteria.

I needed to get to work very early because of my limited transportation situation. So each morning I would buy a newspaper and settle into the cafeteria on the third floor of the old gray government building where I worked.

I was being bothered by several office "mashers" who had taken to coming by the cafeteria to make their advances. Finally I had enough. That morning I picked up my styrofoam cup and paper and approached a table of distinguished looking gentlemen.

"Excuse me, my name is Lois Jacobini and I would appreciate it if I could join your table for coffee," I said. I explained that I was not accustomed to the behavior of my co-workers and I was immediately adopted by the Federal Power Commission's Breakfast Club. Members of the breakfast group included the general counsel, law judges, commissioners, and staff lawyers. These men were responsible for the federal regulation of natural gas.

The thing that puzzled me was that other young ladies would walk by each day, smile, nod and say "Good morning" to everyone. Why didn't they join us? They limited themselves by not having enough confidence and initiative to simply come over and introduce themselves. Who said you had to be "important" or "influential" to sit with this bunch. The Breakfast Club didn't. They would have welcomed other new joiners as they welcomed me.

One day I received a call from the general counsel of the Power Commission, one of our breakfast group members. "Would you be able to have lunch in my office tomorrow to discuss a confidential business matter?" "Of course," I replied. And lunch it was — at his conference table — an Italian sub from a nearby deli.

He told me he was leaving the Commission to work for the reelection of President Nixon. He indicated he had been tremendously impressed with me during our morning breakfast conversations and would I be interested in joining him in the campaign as his administrative assistant.

This posed quite a dilemma for me. My government job, albeit a menial one, was steady and secure. It allowed me to get quickly home to relieve my son's babysitter and was providing me enough income to survive. My potential new boss stressed that following the election I would be on my own. He could make no promise of any kind of job in or out of government. And then I also had to face the fact that I had absolutely no experience whatsoever in politics and as he outlined the job my principal responsibility would be to run the show on a day-to-day basis while he was out of town traveling extensively through his assigned states.

But I had the faith in myself that I could handle the proposed new assignment and I had my belief that change and forward motion are always for the good.

So it was toodles to government service . . . hello campaign trail.

On to Politics . . . On to Power

A political campaign is tough work. The women in my division were the 'creme de la creme'. They had straight access to the White House. In fact, they didn't just know power, they were part of the power. And there I was: 95 pounds, polyester dress two inches above my knees, thrown into the political arena. The key to survival in that atmosphere was to adapt, and this I did quickly. It didn't take me long to figure out the sophisticated dress codes and how to get my job done.

Soon I was briefing White House aides and cabinet level surrogate speakers on the political climate and specific local issues before they would go into the states to rally the support of the people. Thirteen hour days were nothing —issues, internal power struggles, buttons, bumper stickers, the works!

The work was exhausting but exhilarating. It was very hard on me as a mother with the long hours keeping me away from Billy, but I was usually able to steal a few hours a day with him and to somehow get home to share dinner and tuck him in bed—even if it meant coming back to the office to work until daylight. Somehow we both survived the experience.

Election night came quickly. It was a huge bash with lots of tears and the overwhelming feeling of it's all over. The campaign family would spread into a zillion places with nothing left but the packing up. I was out of work again.

As we were cleaning up, again I was invited to have lunch with my boss. He said he was going to work for a Texas law firm, Baker & Botts, and asked if I would like to help him set up the new Washington office of the firm. After the office was opened I could either handle administration work or become his paralegal (legal assistant). I would thus be the first and "pilot" person to be hired by Baker & Botts as a legal assistant.

Again the dilemma. I had found I could return to the safety of government service. My old job was available at the Post Office. What did I know about the law or law firms? But again it was a step forward while the Post Office position would clearly have been looking back.

Toodles campaign . . . hello law firm.

Don't You Want to be the Best in D.C.?

This new job challenge came from the gentlemen in the government cafeteria don't forget! It all stemmed from a single action taken to avoid being harassed by some annoying men. Just *having the courage* to introduce myself to a table of strangers had led me to the White House and now a major downtown law firm. That's not luck. We all have a chance to meet thousands of people in our lifetime. But how do you know until you meet them. Of course they won't all play a significant role in our lives. But the more people you meet, just based on simple percentages, you know your chances improve.

One thing was clear though from the first day of this job: if I didn't create something substantive for myself, my "legal assistant" role would eventually phase into the job of lackey—getting coffee, doing all the copying and routine "go-fer" work.

So I sort of invented a paralegal role for myself. The first thing I did was prepare a daily energy report based on current readings of major newspapers, press releases, and congressional material with follow-up phone calls and investigation for additional between-the-lines input. After a few days of preparing the report my boss came to me and said, "My child, I appreciate this daily report, but you simply don't have to do this."

"Gordon," I asked, "did you know everything in this report?" "No," he replied. "Do you want to be the best lawyer in town?" I asked. Being at that time one of the most revered lawyers in D.C. he was a bit astonished by my question but responded affirmatively. "Then I shall continue preparing my reports."

And that was the end of the discussion. Soon after that and to this day, that *Daily Report* which I invented as a means of keeping my boss informed is disseminated to major Baker & Botts clients and they are charged thousands of dollars a month for it.

My boss would often say, "You have far exceeded my expectations." But in reality this was true only because seldom does anyone receive more than mediocrity; thus, mediocrity has become the norm. I realized I could be the most competent in my field with the exertion of a little more time, energy and creativity. It didn't matter what he expected of me, *what mattered was my own desire to strive for excellence.* And it paid off!

I began to be included in meetings in the stately law firm conference room with heads of major oil companies that had come to Washington to get the behind-the-scenes scoop. How likely is this bill to pass the Senate? Who will try to block? Does it have much support in the House? What parliamentary procedures are expected to be used to force a vote? What trade-offs were made with the White House to get certain amendment support?

I usually had the answers and the firm's clients began to develop a great respect for my knowledge of the political system and its players. But I must admit it didn't come easy for me. I had to first educate myself on the intricacies of energy lawmaking plus the administration and congressional procedures. I was digging and probing and reading and comparing stories every single day in order to stay on top of things.

By the third year, I was among the highest paid paralegals in the country. Sitting there in my private office with tons of "status" symbols (the finest navy leather high-back chair, Williamsburg drapes, a half-dozen research assistants, my own private library, and two secretaries), I would endlessly argue with myself.

"This is wonderful," I'd think. Status, security, a great paycheck and an expense account. But my mind would always race forward with visions of my own research firm carrying out many of the same functions I was now doing for the law firm's clients.

But then I would think that I have a child to raise and that I would have to be crazy to walk away from all this security. And yet I looked on the formation of my own company as a major step of personal growth and confidence based on previous competence. It's called believing in yourself enough to accept that there is more, and to reach out for it instead of being trapped by the personal comforts of familiarity and habit. It is looking forward and not behind.

Toodles to security . . . hello unknown.

Lonely at the Top

When I announced my decision to my parents they expressed all the faith in the world in me, but reminded me that at least eighty percent of all new businesses fold. My mother had urged me not to pursue my company unless I could accept the possibility of failure based on national statistics. I exlained to her that I would rather fall flat on my face than not to try to do something I knew I could do.

The day I resigned from Baker & Botts I went to a small bank to see about getting a line-of-credit. The meeting was set up with the bank president. I talked with him about my new concept of establishing a political research firm on energy matters. The president asked a few questions like: "Do you have any clients?"

"No."

"Do you have any money?"

"No."

I simply responded, "I don't know what is required of me financially, but I do know my business and I know that I'm the best at it and people need my services."

After a few more questions the banker politely explained to me that he should have kicked me out of his office by now, but that he appreciated my honesty and my initiative.

Now I'll let you in on another secret I have learned over the years: If you don't know something, or need help, don't be afraid to ask. I simply said to the banker, "Why don't you tell me what I need to do?" I reached in my bag and pulled out a pad and pen. I nodded, signaling that I was ready. He said that first you need this and then that. I told him I would be back in two weeks.

I returned to the bank with a loan proposal precisely documented. I left the material with the president's secretary. Before noon the next day the bank opened the Washington Experts account with a respectable line of credit and I was in business.

Right then I knew that growth alone made it worthwhile to explore on my own. Clients came in, but slowly. The early stages of business consisted of many late payments. I would anxiously be waiting for my receivables so I could pay rent. The time I received a brief note from a favorite client which read, "We appreciate the fine work that you have done, but we no longer need your services," I felt like crying.

For the first time the thought of "failure" had crept in. I realized that the only way I could maintain my business was to think positively and know that with my skill and desire to succeed it might take time, but I could do it.

Thankfully this phase of my new business was mercifully brief. Gradually, week by week, our client list grew and we began to prosper. It was no longer a matter of life and death whether a check was in today's mail and I could begin to relax, concentrate on turning out a superior work product for my clients and, most importantly, devote more time to my growing son.

Toodles to financial insecurity . . . hello material success.

Energy Powerhouse

Yet as my company continued to grow and grow, I began to realize that simply getting bigger and adding more clients, even though it meant more money, was not really fully satisfying. I came to the most painful realization that I had become a one-dimensional person. I was so busy making sure that I could stand alone that I was alone. I knew that again it was time for change.

That change came when I attended a self-esteem seminar in 1977. I went on a lark thinking that if I had any more self esteem I would be dangerous. What I didn't realize is how frighteningly true that statement was. I was "dangerous" because, as I soon saw, my life so far had been built on faulty values. All I had done was based on negative motivation. My substantial material success had been built on a fear that I would not be accepted, guilt that I had let my parents down, and as a compensation for my embarrassment that I didn't get a formal education. I saw that much of what I was doing was being done to compensate for my lack of sound self-esteem.

When I discovered that I could accept myself and others without condition or judgment the burden of life was gone. From that pearl of principles came the potentiality for my life to soar. It gave me the freedom to create and live my life to the fullest—the way I want. My whole life changed.

It has been said that within the human body is enough electromagnetic energy to blow up an area the size of Washington, D.C. I believe that other people are exploding inside with fear, and guilt, and a sense of no self-worth. I believe personal negative energy, while often a primary motivation for material success, is the number one impediment to self-fulfillment.

But energy, whether physical or metaphysical, cannot be destroyed; only converted into other forms. Negative can be changed into positive. Within each of us is a power-house of a virtually untapped source of potential positive energy.

And as negative energy is transformed into the positive, the potential to revitalize the human body and spirit is beyond comprehension.

Toodles to a frantic sense of urgency . . . hello inner peace.

Success to the Highest

This time the change involved balancing, reshaping, and shifting some of my priorities and values. I decided to keep my company a manageable size so that I would not have to spend hours a day at administrative tasks. I knew that I wanted to share my experiences and my hard learned lessons with others in the hope that others could learn from my story.

Public speaking for me is a means of reaching out to people and sharing the Pearl of Potentiality which I have caught. By devoting my extra time to sharing with others I am able to reenergize my own life. I have found that I can move and affect an audience to positive change and they in turn can touch the lives of those around them by carrying the message of change and positive self-esteem.

As I said in the beginning, "toodles" for me has not meant goodbye, simply change. All that has been a part of me remains a part of me and my level of awareness.

But sometimes in order to continue our forward motion at our own speed and direction, we find ourselves saying "toodles" to our present surroundings, friends, lovers, and family members. It is amazing, though, how often these places and people show up in our life's journey further down the path with more significance than ever.

Sometimes we find ourselves at intersections or detours which appear to be the long route or perhaps completely off course. I believe that no one can ever be off course. For every action I have taken has brought me to the here and now. With every step of my life comes new understanding and growth, and unexplored potential.

My goal, my purpose, is to share what I have learned and to give more love and energy than possible in just one lifetime. I take life a step at a time but always maintain perpetual motion. This method for my life brings me closer and closer to my horizon, where all aspects of my life come together in harmony.

I chart my life each day as new ideas and opportunities unfold. My guide comes from within me and I listen. When it signals I take action. By accepting myself and trusting God I have total freedom to move toward my heart's desires. Never standing still; never looking back. *Being alive and present to each moment takes my potential success to the highest levels and it will do the same for you.*

Your personal feedback would be appreciated. Please contact me at:

1211 Connecticut Ave. #403
Washington, DC. 20036

Rebecca Dunn
2995 L.B.J. Fwy. Suite 115
Dallas, TX 75234
(214) 620-0172

REBECCA DUNN

Rebecca Dunn is a successful, dynamic woman possessing a diverse and exciting background in lecturing, administration, public relations, legislation, management, secondary education, writing, and prisoner rehabilitation.

As an associate of Executive Development Systems of Dallas, Texas, Rebecca conducts personal development seminars for executives and possesses additional expertise in planning workshops and programs for educators and teenagers.

Graduating from the University of South Dakota, Rebecca continued graduate study in History, English, and American Studies at the Universty of Hawaii and received a Master of Arts in English and American Literature.

At the age of 23, with $130.00 in hand, she relinquished the cloister of education and hitchhiked, studied, and worked at odd jobs in Europe, Africa and Asia for two years. This creative, spontaneous, adventurous period was enormously valuable in developing her awareness and sensitivity toward others.

Rebecca is an impelling speaker on the topic of "You Are What You Think." By nurturing the mind through selective reading, viewing and listening, the quality of one's thinking improves, thereby enhancing one's life. She has conducted motivational seminars for inmates in the South Dakota State Penitentiary and is presently an Instructor with Dale Carnegie and Associates in Dallas, Texas.

An enthusiast of running, swimming, scuba diving, and yoga, Rebecca believes in the power of positive thought to effect one's own circumstances and character.

A slow trot in a fast race cannot win. But if oneself and things are set into movement, mistakes can be overcome, achievements become possible.
TAO

YOUR THOUGHTS — YOUR PEARLS!

by Rebecca Dunn

Reaching Out

We sat by the side of the road in Southern France thinking out loud, talking about where we would hitch a ride today. My friend, hunched over a large map of Europe, said, "Let's go to Paris." As I tore apart bread and sliced cheese and tomatoes for our morning breakfast, I thought about the suggestion. The time was right. We had not been to a city for nearly a month. Art galleries, opera, and the electric vibrations of the city sounded appealing. Suddenly, a Rolls Royce pulled to a stop across the road. A young man leaned his head out of the window and shouted, "Wanna go to Istanbul?" My friend and I exchanged a by-now familiar 'Why Not?' look. Scooping up our gear and half-eaten breakfast, we were off to an adventure in Turkey!

Recognize, accept and enjoy your opportunities! All of us seeking successful living know the importance of goal setting, outlining on paper and engraving in our minds our purpose, our goal. During our quest for this goal, it is vital to enjoy life . . . take a side trip to Istanbul! By doing this, we keep things in perspective. Our goal is still achieved and more pleasurably.

Just Luck?

A girlfriend from college sorority days when seeing me sometimes will say, "Becky, you are so lucky!"

"Why?"

"Oh, everything neat just naturally happens to you. You lived in Hawaii and you have traveled all over the world. You have so many adventures!"

When she and others say this, I am usually flattered but also a little amused. Why? Because I believe that you make your own luck!

Growing up in Sioux Falls, South Dakota, I had watched people go away, travel, and come back with souvenirs and exciting stories. I loved going out to the tiny municipal airport with my Daddy and wait and wait until the one airplane scheduled to arrive that night would land. I wanted to see the world too, experience the cultures of other peoples, live as they did, try to see life from someone else's point of view. Tired of reading *National Geographic,* I wanted to live it!

People often are intrigued when they hear of my travels hitchhiking and working at odd jobs in Europe, Africa, and Asia for two years. Invariably, someone will say, however, "Is it really true that you went over there with only $130.00?" The answer is "Yes!" If I hadn't, I would probably still be saving to have the "proper" amount of money! Frankly, if I waited until I had enough money to do things, I probably never would do anything! As it was, I wanted to go *then*. My courageous Mother trusted and encouraged me from Day #1. I was not afraid to work hard and besides I wanted to travel among the people of the countries, sleep in their lodges (and in their fields). I wanted to feel a part of another culture, as much as a foreigner can feel a part of a place that belongs to someone else. While working in Amsterdam at the Krasnopolsky Hotel cleaning bathrooms, I watched American tourists. Sometimes their attitude and behavior was shocking, at other times delightful. People assumed I was Dutch as I scrubbed in my pinafore uniform pushing my blonde braids back. The amazing discovery was that as I learned about Holland and America, I was also learning so much about myself. As we widen our world of perspective, we widen our view of ourselves. That "career" lasted about a month and I moved on to something else . . . another country, another adventure, another perspective.

Granted there were times when I only saw one-half an opera because the cheapest seats were so high and so far to the side that I viewed only half the stage. But I slept in caves in Crete, Prince Ranier's palace grounds in Monaco, grape vineyards in Italy, a shoemaker's shop in Budapest, and the homes of the people all over the world.

A Taste of Beauty

The lovely benefit I received was a taste of something delicious . . . a taste of the beauty of life. This is a significant point: do not limit your goals and dreams because you do not think you have the money! You really can do what you wish if you want it badly enough. You *can* create your own opportunities!

Reaching In

"A man's mind is the man himself."

Latin Proverb

One of the secrets of life is to be ready when an opportunity comes. Therefore, it is imperative that you send out
electric, positive energy so that people notice you and *offer*
you opportunities! How does this happen? I think 'like
attracts like.' People of enthusiasm, integrity and justice
attract others like themselves.

When conducting seminars and classes, my emphasis
always revolves around one issue: nurture your own
thinking process everyday! Be selective about what you
read, to what you listen, to what you observe. Be attentive
in what you allow to filter into your mind and settle there!
How careful most of us are in selecting what we eat,
examining closely the food in the market and selecting the
freshest meat and produce. Are we as solicitous in protecting and nurturing our minds?

When I read the newspapers and magazines, I am on
guard. Reading critically, I get the facts and leave the gory
sensational details. My mind and my time are special so I
want to pack as much quality "meat" into my mind just as
into my body. To do this, an hour or two a week is spent
browsing Taylor's Bookstore in Dallas selecting next
reading projects. Reading allows my imagination to flow
into another time period, another's life, another's thought
process. I read about people I admire, how they lived, what
their priorities were. Some of them have been Justice
William O. Douglas, Abraham Lincoln, Theodore
Roosevelt, Rose Kennedy, Henry David Thoreau, and
Anne Morrow Lindbergh. Mrs. Lindbergh especially has
been a source of inspiration. Her constant quest to keep
quality perspective impresses me. It was a continuing
challenge to combine a meaningful private family life
with her husband and children, yet to maintain her integrity as a professional writer and her personal life as a
woman. In all of her diaries and books, I felt this keenly,
this urgent need to fulfill these separate selves and the
complexities she encountered in doing so. By reading how
others have worked through their opportunities, I receive
strength and courage to face my own. By feeding my mind

with positive constructive ways to make changes, I deal with my own problems as challenges and opportunities.

Selective Listening

Just as meaningful as selective reading in nurturing our thought process is selective listening. Does the music you enjoy soothe you, lift you, enlighten you? Have you known people or family members who immediately upon seeing you begin telling you everything that has gone wrong in their life since they last saw you? You feel it is almost their duty to keep you updated on the negatives in their lives . . . the wife telling her husband all that has gone wrong as he comes through the door and the husband replying with all that had gone wrong at the office! If your back is stiffening, stop and listen to yourself! What kind of attitude and image are you presenting to the world? Are people happy to see you? Are you giving off positive energy that attracts people to you or are you someone people would like to avoid because you are the bearer of Bad News?

People often ask me if Ed Foreman, the President of Executive Development Systems, is always as positive and cheerful as he appears when he is speaking before conventions and conducting seminars around the country. The answer is an enthusiastic "Yes!" Here is his secret. He always starts a conversation with this question: "What good things are going on with you today?" Anyone that knows Ed or sees him coming is already rolling the positive thoughts through their minds or they are going to be at a loss for words! Sometimes he stops people short! But he makes people think! Each conversation is positive and likewise are conferences and meetings if started in this absolute way. If you want to create opportunities or if you want to be noticed for your talents and intelligence, make sure you are projecting a positive outlook on life and are the person to whom someone would like to offer an opportunity!

No Rubbish Allowed

Just as we have a choice in what we read and to what we listen, we also have choices in viewing. All of us are aware of the power of film and television in capturing the attention of children. There is an opportunity for constant inspiration, creative education, and excellent entertainment! Unfortunately, the mind often is not educated, inspired, or entertained but rather mesmerized, dulled and even decayed. Just as we should be careful not to let others dump their complaining rubbish into our minds, so too should we be careful not to watch rubbish either. Our bodies are exactly what we feed them and so are our minds. We are a reflection of the seeds we plant and nurture within ourselves. We can control what goes into our minds just as we can control what we take into our bodies.

We have many choices and many alternatives in life. We live only one life. There is good and bad in much that we read, listen to and observe. Eleanor Roosevelt said, "In the long run, we shape our lives and we shape our destinies. The process never ends until we die. And the choices we make are ultimately our own responsibility." By being selective, we can take the best from everyone we meet, everything we read or listen to and place the best context on it in reference to our own lives. By doing this, we nurture our minds preparing ourselves to create opportunities or be exciting individuals that will be offered opportunities. We are what we think about all day long. If we lift up our thoughts, so we will lift up ourselves.

Feel the Joy!

While caring for the mind is a properly developed habit, so too is the caring for one's body. I swim laps, do yoga, and run. Really, it doesn't matter what exercise you do as long as you do something! Your relief from tension and anxiety, your peace of mind and inner security depend upon it! For we women, exercise is not always thought of as pleasurable. Pant! Pant! However, a Plan has been devised to make it pleasurable! It happened by accident one day while I was running. Having run about a mile, my calves in both legs began to cramp. I was determined to get my run in, no matter what, so I did the following: As the cramps got worse, I started saying to myself, "Feel the joy and release the pain. Feel the joy of running and release the pain of running!" This I said over and over. What happened was the immediate start of a positive thought process that emphasized *why* I was running in the first place! I thought of my slimmer body and legs; I thought how great it was to run faster and longer than when I was 15; I thought how good the fresh air felt on my skin and rushing through my hair; I thought how wonderful it was to have two healthy legs and to be able to run at all; I felt grateful to be alive on this beautiful day! Well, with all that positive thought, I ran twice around the golf course! I regularly use that positive thought process when I feel sluggish during my exercise program. More significantly, I use it when I need to get "psyched" up to get out there and *do it!*

Hawaii Nokaoi*

For several years I lived in Hawaii, first as a governess while attending graduate school at the University of Hawaii. Later I managed the E. L. Doheny Estate on Diamond Head and was an instructor at the famed Punahou College Preparatory Academy in Honolulu. During that first year as a governess for the children of Sandy and Jackolyn Gadient, I experienced the demands of trying to be student and mother! All four of the children were under the age of seven. Cranking out a comparative study between Faulkner and Hemmingway at 2:00 a.m. after reading Winnie the Pooh a few hours earlier was pretty normal

*Hawaiian — "The very best"

procedure! A few hours later, I would be up at 6:00, fixing lunches, projects and hair and then getting them off to school. By 9:00, it was necessary to be parked on campus (in Hawaii?!) and in class! Importantly during this time in Hawaii, I fell in love with the sea. I came to terms with my own varying emotions taking long early walks on the beach with one of the children and watching Gary Nokaoi, age 2, tumble down to the shore pulling off his diapers so they wouldn't get "wet." By gazing at a seashell or peering into a small coral pool, I enlarged my perspective by narrowing it. That night I would be in a seminar discussing the tragedies of Shakespeare and the social, political, and economic implications of his works. But on the beach, I could perhaps come closest to myself. To this day, life is better when there is a child in my life, when I am taking a class, when I am near the sea.

Many successful women overcome obstacles by necessity. In retrospect, I realize that I often created obstacles to test myself, my strength, my ability, my courage. I do not emerge from a background of hardship yet I yearn for many levels of experience and existence.

Stand Your Ground!

One of my most growing experiences was my term in the South Dakota State Prison . . . as an Instructor, that is! When the Warden, Herm Solem, offered me the position as a member of an experimental program under Title I, I was both excited and scared to death! At the time, my father was the Chief Justice of the Supreme Court of South Dakota, and for obvious reasons it would be necessary to keep the fact that I was his daughter quiet! The deathly chill that crept over me as I walked up to that sinister granite building that first day and the ensuing feelings of entrapment as the automatic gates started closing behind me shall never be forgotten. Each step further into the interior of the prison took me further from my security, my comfort zone. I was more afraid than I had been scaling cliffs in the dark to reach my cave on the island of Crete! Here I would be working with men who had murdered, robbed, raped . . . men who had committed the most violent of crimes.

When I was introduced to Ray, one of my students, the first thing he said to me was this: "I am a dummy. I have been a dummy all of my life. You may as well not even try with me."

As the days went by and I worked tentatively with them, I knew that they too were afraid. Afraid they could do the work, afraid they could not, afraid to try, afraid not to, afraid someone might get ahead of them, afraid they might have to take risks and change. Generally the obvious low self-esteem possessed by the inmates was overwhelming. Most of them felt that they were worth nothing. Someone at home or at school had told them indirectly or directly this all of their lives. All of the men were under 30 years of age. It was tragic and I was empathetic. How grateful I was that my own parents had been such a positive, encouraging force in my life! Yet, no matter how tragic their experiences were, I do not believe it helps to go through life being sad, angry, or apathetic because one never was presented the "opportunity" of a nice education, a nice job, or a nice home. There were hundreds of men and women outside the prison who had similar horrid experiences yet had turned their negatives into positives and were leading productive lives. It was this sentiment that led to a show-down in the prison one day. I had started the seminar on goal setting beginning with the significance of goal setting in my own life. Then I led into the importance of their setting goals now within the prison so they could make the transition to productive living when they were released. One of the men at the far end of the seminar table yelled, "Aw, what's this goal stuff? Life just happens, man! You can't plan it!"

Another spoke up, "Sure, it's easy for you to say!"

As I glanced around the table at the smirks on their faces and the agreeing consensus of this response, I became angry. The next thing I knew, I was on my feet and had flung one of the texts down on the seminar table and my fist followed.

Move!

"That is *it*! I have *had* it with you guys! You sit here every day expecting someone to hand you a terrific life and grumble in your misery because this is not a country club! You have violated society and yet you act like society should do you the favor! No one, including me, is going to do you any favors until you start doing them for yourselves. *That* starts with planning and goal setting and thinking about the changes you want to make in your own life. I am here to assist you in bringing about the changes . . . good grief, it is not for the money or the benefits! Now those of you that want to work with me toward improving your future, just pick up your chairs and move down to the end of the room and the rest of you can just get out!"

Scanning the back of the room that was encased in glass, I suddenly noticed all the guards standing there looking like they were ready to move in! They had to be wondering what in the world had come over me! But still, glaring back at the men I continued: "I have never meant anything more in my life!"

One man got up and walked out immediately. The other 19 slowly picked up their chairs and moved a few feet down to the end of the room. From that moment on, they knew I was serious in my intent to work with them, to show them an alternative way. Perhaps I gained their respect. From then on there was a productive buzz in the classroom. Ray, who had been tested at a 3rd grade competency level and had said he was a "dummy" on the first day, received his GED within the year. I still work with Ray and I am confident that he is going to make it on the outside.

I do not suggest this type of confrontation but I do not think we should allow ourselves to be intimidated! While people may not agree with our strong convictions, they will listen if we are serious in our intent to help them. Freedom lies in being bold! And we cannot be free if we cannot go to the end of our thoughts.

Had I been crippled by my early shallow fears, had I not stood my ground in my belief that the men could create a positive future for themselves, I would have lost an opportunity to assist Ray and the others.

Let Us Never Be A Cold and Timid Soul

Fear and fear of failure hold so many people back from stretching out and doing the things they so desperately want to do. How many opportunities are missed because of fear! Nothing I have read has ever touched me quite like Theodore Roosevelt's answer to conquering fear.

"It is not the critic who counts; not the man who points out how the strong man stumbled, or where the doer of deeds could have done better. The credit belongs to the man who is actually in the arena; whose face is marred by dust and sweat and blood; who strives valiantly; who errs and comes short again and again; who knows the great enthusiasms, the great devotions, and spends himself in a worthy cause; who at the best knows in the end the triumph of high achievement; and who at the worst, if he fails, at least fails while daring greatly; so that his place shall never be with those cold and timid souls who know neither victory nor defeat."

Even if we fail, we can turn that experience into an opportunity! Any time I encounter a painful, difficult, or "failing" situation, I immediately begin asking myself, What have I learned here? Why has this happened? How can I grow from this experience? By doing this I treat my experience as a failure and not myself. Precious self esteem is not damaged, but rather enhanced because I have learned to face failure and deal with it in a positive way.

After each fall, merely analyze your mistakes and set about to ready these imperfections.

I never want to say, 'I wish I had done that,' and hadn't because I thought I would fail if I tried. My own personal setbacks have set me on the launching pad of a rewarding life! I am amazed at what I can do with my own resources! Without dealing with the adversity in my life, I would not have the strength, courage and drive that I possess today. Our strength is the product of our struggles. Besides a great happiness comes through victory . . . victory in addressing a fear, conquering it, laying it to rest. George Bernard Shaw said: "A life spent in making mistakes is not only more honorable but more useful than a life spent in doing nothing." If we have done our best, given our best, and still failed, we are still rewarded in knowing that we shall never be "one of those cold and timid souls who know neither victory nor defeat."

Pearls of Potentiality

While growing up in South Dakota, my brothers, David and Tom, and my sister Carol and I were never given everything my parents never had. However we were presented opportunities to get what we wanted from a very early age. David and Tom have both worked since they were young boys, at first selling newspapers. Both are successful attorneys today. Carol and I were babysitting and working at the Dairy Queen in our early teens. My parents always provided money for any lessons or trips in which we were interested. As a result of this early emphasis of expanding experiences and awareness, these are my values today. Justice William O. Douglas once said that the character of man is not only measured by looking at what he is doing when he is 60 or 65 but also by examining what occupied his interests when he was 17 or 19.

A creed I try to live by was written by Ralph Waldo Emerson when he was asked, "What do you expect from life?"

"To laugh often and love much, to win the respect of
intelligent persons and the affection of children; to
earn the approbation of honest critics; to appreciate
beauty; to give one's self, to leave the world a bit
better, whether by a healthy child, a garden patch,
or a redeemed social condition; to have looked for the
best in others and given them the best we had; to
know even one life has breathed easier because we
lived . . ."

Every experience in life is an opportunity. The greatest
use of life is to spend it for something that will outlast it.
To accomplish great things, we must have a plan and a
belief. To carry out this plan, we must nurture our minds
and bodies, discovering the adventure within, so that we
are valuable to ourselves as well as to others. Life is a
lovely journey and a daring adventure which begins and
ends with the peace we create within ourselves. We must
always be ready to exchange what we are for what we can
become.

Lorneva Johnson
500 W. 16th St.
National City, CA 92050
(714) 477-2738

LORNEVA JOHNSON

Lorneva Johnson is president and "Granny" of H&L Products, Inc., member of the Automotive Parts and Accessories Association, associate member of the American Research Merchandising Institute, and manufacturer of Granny brand auto convenience accessories. Several of these are the best selling of their kind.

Growing up in the Ozark foothills, Lorneva developed an inventive mind and a dawn to dark work ethic she still employs. As a girl her hobby was collecting Indian arrowheads and artifacts and she still today enjoys rockhounding trips with her husband Howard. In the small town of Hector, Arkansas she was captain of the girls basketball team and still takes on anyone at free-throws in the patio of her Spanish Villa in the beautiful resort city of Coronado, California.

Lorneva was recognized by the San Diego Ad Club with high mention in local media. A topical article recently appeared in Money magazine about her Squeeze Play Pocket Ashtray which now has a patent pending on its invention.

She was the innovator of the running tuck sewing method now employed by many bag makers and Lorneva has designed products currently sold by Schwinn, Pitney Bowes, as well as her own Luraline Handbag Totes and Easy Rider Bike Accessories.

Lorneva feels blessed to have all her four children and their families in the area and makes sure that each birthday turns into a grand occasion.

She is a grand deaconess in the Graham Memorial Presbyterian Church where she has been a member for thirty-five years and has always been interested in community affairs.

The journey of a thousand miles begins with one step.
LAO-TSZE

GRANNY'S BAG IS BAGS

by Lorneva Johnson

Three big trucks were loading the day's shipments and I visualized for a moment their destinations. I thought of the many cities and towns all over our great country and felt proud that some of the thirty-six products my factory made were in most of them. In fact, every seven seconds of every business day, someone somewhere is buying a Granny brand item. Having good products for people to enjoy is really rewarding, just like baking a good apple pie and having guests ask for seconds. But you know, although millions of our convenience accessories such as litter bags, eyeglass caddies, visor devices, tool cases, door pockets, fender covers, and tissue holders are in cars all over the world, the start was an idea and a single little litter bag I sewed one evening at home.

My friends have often asked me, "Did you ever think your business would be so big, so successful?" I usually just smile, but the real answer would be, "Yes! Yes, I did."

Pictures In The Mind

From the very start I rented the largest post office box available to hold all the mail H&L would be getting. I had a mental picture of my litter bags being sold in every store and could just see the people going in to buy them. I could almost feel the nice soft vinyl I'd use, hear the sewing machines humming, and see the merchandise arriving at the stores in white boxes just as perfectly as it left the factory. My picture was vivid in my mind but at first I was like an artist who couldn't mix the paint or even hold the brush.

I suppose parts of my picture began forming several years ago. I was working part time selling advertising and the extra money was just great. I could buy those little extras for my four children and still have time with my family. Each month though, before handing out the checks, Dottie Walters would tell us how to sell our advertising. She would cover points later included in her marvelous book, *Never Underestimate the Selling Power of a Woman.* "Find the need and fill it, someone is just *waiting* for you," she would say. But she must be talking to the others, I would think. I was working part time just to make a little extra money, not really *interested* in sales. Then one day after the meeting, she handed me my monthly check, then drew it back, looked me in the eye and said, "Is *this* all the money you want to make? You know you write your *own* check and others with only half your *potential* have written themselves checks for four times as much." She handed me the check and, as I looked at the amount of $228, Dottie said, "Is that all you think you're worth?"

Just as I started to get angry, I remembered some of her words. You are your own boss. Your own manager. Set goals. Plan your time. Get organized. Maybe she *had* been talking to me all the time! I could hardly wait to get home, get organized, plan, set goals. That's just what I did. I accomplished more, got more satisfaction, had more time with my family, and my paychecks were soon the highest in the company.

Keep Score

But money wasn't really the goal. Selling advertising was. Even now that we have a beautiful home, inflated now to a half million in value, own our modern factory and the block where it is located, money in itself has never been a goal. I know many unhappy people with lots of money. The dollars are a way of keeping score. *There's nothing quite so rewarding as achieving a goal that you've set for yourself,* no matter what it may be.

After deciding I was going to *really sell* advertising it became fun. I called on new businesses every day and made many new friends. Pretty soon I developed the ability to walk in, stop for a moment, look at the expressions on people's faces and most always see which person I should be talking to. These persons *were* the business. Of course many businesses failed. But so many others really prospered. Ralph Nader once said that 80% of business is controlled by 200 large corporations. Some say bigness is what counts these days and small business doesn't have a chance. But I've seen many in my calls in advertising where owners and executives have turned their own ideas into *Pearls of Potentiality*. They formed their own pictures of where they wanted to be and their faces mirrored their motivation to achieve their goals. I saw small cafes become restaurant chains, small offices become large agencies, and many whose goals are realized. Free enterprise is alive and well and after seeing so much of it first hand, I made up my mind that, at fifty years of age, I was going to own my own business. I just didn't know what, when, or how.

A Flash From The Trash

Driving around San Diego as much as two hundred miles in one day, I soon needed a new car. It was such a thrill to open the door, smell the newness, and slide behind the wheel. It was such a beautiful car it just had to stay that way. It seemed like almost every other day I was buying a new litter container or basket to keep everything looking clean, fresh and new. But nowhere could I find one that really pleased me and looked good. Then one day I happened to be in an upholstery shop and the idea came to me of a litterbag made of the same material as the upholstery. How perfect! I bought a piece of expanded vinyl that matched my car and that night I made my litterbag. To me it was beautiful but I didn't expect everyone who rode in my car to want one like it. When they would ask where I bought it I'd always answer proudly, "I made it." With this new bag in place, and enjoying the comments, I soon became interested in litter control and joined the San Diego Anti-Litter Committee. Highway litter was then an even bigger problem than it is today. One Friday afternoon as I was driving home on highway 94, at peak traffic, a car full of young people passed me and just as they were a few feet ahead, the young man threw a sack full of trash out the window. Most of it landed on my windshield and with the crack of what seemed to be a metal object, I swerved, almost hitting another car. After regaining my composure I kept glancing at the litter bag I'd made and the picture in my mind became clearer, and clearer.

I was glad when I reached home that evening, Howard, my husband was there, I wanted to tell him of my idea for our litter bag business. He had already settled down to a good book and to my surprise, he put it down to listen, with interest. He asked where the bag was and went out to the car to get it. He brought it in and said, "It still looks new! I can't believe you've used it almost two years. What's the first thing you need?"

Granny's Bag

Saturday morning, we shopped for an industrial sewing machine. I wanted to start with a used one, but Howard's Norwegian dad had told him when he was a young man, "Don't just buy a hat. Buy a Stetson." So we bought the very best and biggest sewing machine in the store. Then we stopped at a wholesale warehouse and bought a bare minimum of beautiful vinyl in six different colors. The man still remembers that day when we told him we were going to manufacture litter bags. We asked him for his best prices, told him we would soon be using truckloads, and then took two yards of each color. He seemed a little skeptical of our plans, to say the least. We got home, put the machine in the bedroom, and plugged it in. I hadn't planned on *me* sewing. I quickly cut out a litterbag and turned on the machine. The stitches were good but I didn't know how to make it stop. I quickly unplugged it, but it kept on sewing. It came unthreaded and I didn't know how to thread it back. After an hour of frustration, I remembered that my daughter, Willette, had been taking an upholstery class at school. She came over, and with my directions and her sewing, we made the first bag, with a real industrial sewing machine. The following Saturday evening we were having dinner with my son Denny, my daughter-in-law Bonnie, and my grand-daughter Amy who was then just nine months old. I wanted to share our enthusiasm for our new business and we talked about names for the new litter bag. We hunted for a name almost all through dinner. I was so pleased that Amy could use her spoon so well, as I sat across from her with a grand-mother's sparkle. Bonnie said, "Amy, Granny sure loves you," and in her next breath said, "That's it! Call it Granny's bag."

I did know we had to have a business license, but when the woman at city hall asked me, "What's the name of your company?", I said, "Granny Litter Bags," She looked up at me and slowly shook her head. "You don't *really* want that for a name, do you? What if you decide to do something else." I thought that over for a minute, noticed the line behind me and her fingers tapping on the counter, and decided on our first two initials, H&L. H&L Manufacturing Company was in business.

The Chinese have a saying that a journey of a thousand miles begins with but a single step. That single first shortens the distance we have to travel to our goal and it confirms our hope and renews our faith that we have earnestly embarked on our journey.

What If?

But there are few roadmaps for the highway to success. I went to the library, gathered and read biographies of successful people, sought advice from others in business and ordered booklets from the Small Business Administration. But much of it was about as helpful as the directions a man jokingly got when he asked how to get to Chicago from San Diego. He was told to go up the road apiece to University Avenue, turn right and when he got to Texas, to bear a little to his left until he got there. It's really hard to apply platitudes and generalities when it comes to the everyday working of a business. I didn't know they would want a sales tax deposit when I had no sales. I didn't know a store would require a million dollar liability insurance before considering purchase of a litter bag. Workman's comp, Quarterly reports to the State, Withholding, Unemployment Insurance, journals, ledgers, guarantees, cash discounts, freight allowances, case cubes . . . whew! The list was endless. Then when it came to selling . . . "Pay for litter bags? We give those away!", or even worse, "What's a litter bag?" The more I learned, the more I found out how much more there was to know. It didn't matter that my litter bags sold well in a few small stores. Buyers didn't want one product, they wanted a product line. And even when I gave my best price, they wanted even better to meet price points. And the expenses; rent, heat, lights, stationery, postage and the phone, the phone that wouldn't ring!

As we travel through life there are many turns we could have taken and at every junction we wonder, what if? What if we had taken another road? Changing directions is difficult and, too often, we become creatures of habit, doing the familiar, plodding ahead because it's the easiest road to take, afraid that the road to the side will be a detour or dead-end.

After two years my road was getting pretty rough, but I was never afraid I wouldn't reach my goal. You just have to keep on keeping on and sometimes this takes more courage than we know we have.

Show That You're Not Afraid

I remember a lesson my father taught me when I was five just starting school. We had a farm and each day as I started my three-mile walk to school, my dad would have to walk me through the cow pasture because we had a big longhorned bull that would charge at me. He would charge, by lowering his head and pawing the ground, and I could see smoke coming from his huge nostrils. Naturally, I was afraid and wouldn't dare leave without Dad beside me.

One Saturday he said to me, "We're going to keep that bull, and you still have to go to school. I don't want to walk across the pasture with you every day, so we have to do something about the bull." He then turned to me and said, "You go run and get the broom." Then with the broom in hand we marched off to the pasture. Dad said, "You have to show that bull you're not afraid of him and when you do, he will never charge at you again. Go out in the pasture and when he bows up to charge, you run at him with the broom and beat him just as fast and as hard as you can. *Don't ever show you're afraid.* Just keep beating him. I'll stand by so don't run whatever you do." I still remember that going into that cow pasture against that bull took more courage than I thought I had. But with Dad yelling,

"Get him! Get him!," I stayed right in there, just pounding at his eyes until he turned and ran the other way. I can still hear my dad's voice, "You did it! *You did it!*" Just as soon as I got my breath Dad said "Go out this time without the broom and walk toward the bull." So I did, and this time it was the bull that did the running. By showing the bull that I wasn't afraid of him, he became afraid of me. I never worried about that old bull again.

Each problem with the business had to be tackled head-on, one problem at a time, for I found I could always handle that day one day at a time. Soon, with this dogged determination, everyone realized I was serious and wasn't going to quit. Through frequent contact, I got to know the people who could buy. Each little success story of how well one company sold litter bags became a track record I could use for the next.

My family was there helping too, first a little and then a lot, until they became as enthusiastic about the business as I was. My brother, Al Dixon, joined the company and would work at production in the day and write letters at night. Howard, with his attention to detail, analyzed every step of each operation, kept all the records, went with me on calls, and kept us all enthusiastic. He knew the business would be successful from the start. My daughter Lura became our secretary, and even my youngest daughter, Loretta worked along with everyone else. There was always work.

The original Granny Litterbag now has sales over four million. We had end pieces, we turned into glasscases. There were thousands of these already on the market, and our sales were to automotive markets, so we then put a piece of elastic on the case and now this product has sold over two million. Buyers have helped us too with new products and new ideas. From one large automotive account we learned that with glove compartments getting smaller there was a need for a door pocket and the sales are tremendous. When the largest supermarket wanted a bike bag we made one and today we make bags for Schwinn.

Wherever there is a need for a product we ask ourselves if we can make it better. Where before trips to the store were just for personal items, today we are always looking at other products; the design, function, color, price, adaptability, labeling and so many other factors that go with marketing.

We've now emerged from the "cocoon years," and each day brings a new dawn and we look for new horizons. Nothing in the world of business stands still and if we don't go forward we have to fall back. There are always opportunities just waiting, new goals to set, and better things in store.

Each business, each corporation is as individual as a fingerprint. Each started with ideas, the veritable *Pearls of Potentiality* that are tossed to all of us. Everyday we see services that could be better, work that could be done more efficiently, and products that could be improved in some way. We have only to catch these pearls, gather the ideas, form our picture of how it will be and make it so indelible in our minds that nothing can deter us from our goal. No matter what this idea may be, *if we have the motivation and will to succeed, we will.* What the mind can see and believe, we can achieve.

Bobbie Gee
31781 National Park Dr.
South Laguna, CA 92677
(714) 496-3545

BOBBIE GEE

With over twenty years in the fields of grooming, fashion, appearance and motivation, Bobbie Gee has gained a vast and impressive array of credentials. Her professional experiences have taken her from the jungles of the West Indies to the castles of the Magic Kingdom of Disneyland.

Bobbie most recently was responsible for "The Disney Look," conducting training seminars for all levels of Disneyland Management. She had the challenging role of maintaining and supporting the over-all appearance and image of 8000 Disneyland employees. She also served Management as Coordinator of the Disney Corporation's Speakers Bureau.

Prior to Disneyland, Bobbie was Public Relations Director for the John Robert Powers Studio, lecturing to schools, colleges and social clubs throughout Southern California.

Internationally, she spent two years in Trinidad lecturing for groups such as the United Nations Guild, speaking on grooming, fashion and social graces to people from throughout the world.

Bobbie's background includes five years as a Fashion Coordinator. In addition, she has produced, directed and hosted her own television shows and has been owner of a Self-Improvement Studio.

As a motivator and training speaker, Bobbie Gee is the consumate professional. She is a contributing author for several publications and her vibrant personality has been featured in numerous magazine and newspaper articles.

She is a seminar leader and motivator in the field of Visual Image communication having lectured to thousands.

Bobbie is also president and founder of the Orange County Speakers Bureau, representing some of America's foremost speakers.

She and her husband, Ernie, are the parents of two daughters.

One cannot lose what belongs by nature to one, even if one attempts to throw it away. One should strive to be true to one's nature, and not be led astray by the words of others.
TAO

FROM DREAM TO REALITY AT DISNEYLAND

by Bobbie Gee

What a joy and privilege to be asked to share with you the triumphs and failures of my life. Why must we talk about both? Because that is what life is made up of: trying and winning, or trying and failing. I would like to believe that most of your life has been on the winning side. Mine has! Your life started out that way. Has it continued? As a baby you did not say to yourself, "If I try to walk I might fall down. So I'll just stay on the floor where it is safe." No, you tried and tried again until one day there you were on your feet. You truly believed you could do it; there were living examples all around you. We did not start out knowing how to walk, and we do not start out in life with all the knowledge we will have when we die. It's a growing process, a combination of trial and error, success and failure. Both are quite normal. So many people feel everything they do must be a success, and because they fear it won't be, they just don't try. I have always tried to teach my two beautiful daughters that failure is just not trying at all. Do I feel like a winner? Yes I do. Am I a winner? Yes I am. Have I ever failed? More times than I can count. But I just don't think about the failures. I try always to keep my successes foremost in my mind.

My confidence comes from the Bible, the most winning book you could ever own. M. R. Kopmeyer, America's famous success counselor and author of some of our greatest books on success, told me he felt every secret to being a winner was written there-in, and that it was the greatest success book ever written. What a joy it was for me not only to meet this wonderful man, but also to hear his comments on my favorite book.

How could my parents ever have known that, on the February morning, a sweet little 19-inch girl would one day measure in at six feet one-half inch? For me that came sooner than later. I measured six foot before I entered high school, and I have heard every tall joke ever written. Was my physical characteristic to offer me opportunity? I can truthfully say that upon entering high school that I was not only the tallest girl in school, but I was also taller than all my teachers. Many of you might be saying, "That poor girl. It's hard enough just being a teenager, but a six foot one." What many people might feel would be an adverse condition worked just in reverse. I learned I had to try harder, and that I had to try over and over again.

Tall is Terrific

At age 17 I found out that (*tall is terrific*). How lucky I am that the Master of all creation designed this female to measure in at six foot one-half inch. It was all planned long before I was ever born (Psalms 139-13). So was the potential to become a winner. We are all born with it.

My success revolves around my careers in the fashion and personal awareness industry. It is a grand field, as everyone is interested in themselves, and most people are interested in self-improvement in some form or other. I started teaching self-improvement at the age of 15. This came about due to a contest I had won. I, like so many other young girls, wanted to be a model. While in modeling school, I entered a contest and won as the most poised. My high school gym teachers heard about it and asked me to teach the gym classes one day a week. I was asked to teach poise, fashion, modeling or whatever I wanted in the self-improvement field. What an opportunity! But what if I made a fool out of myself? Was life offering me my first real chance at success, or was I setting myself up to be disliked by all the other girls at school? I remember how I wanted to try out for pep squad, but knew in my heart that one six-footer beside five other girls all five-foot six-inch or under just wasn't going to happen. This time, however, it was different. There wouldn't be five other girls all five-foot six-inches to stand next to. Could I do it? Somehow deep inside me I knew I had to try. I must confess to you I absolutely did not know what I was doing, nor did I have any idea what I would say. But that little voice deep inside just kept saying, "You can do it; you can do it!" The fear that swept over me has been felt by so many of you reading this book. This is the danger point. Do I give into my fear or do I accept the strength that God promises me: That He is with me in all things. I accepted the challenge. Many years have passed since my first venture into the public speaking field. Daily I give thanks for parents that introduced me to the promises that if I believe, *all things are possible.*

Shortly after graduation from high school, I was hired, by a lovely lady I very much admired, to teach in one of the nation's largest self-improvement schools. For the next two years this beautiful woman was my mentor. It was like having Beethoven as your piano coach. She told me what I did right, and she was also kind enough to tell me what I did wrong. I am very thankful to the people in my life who have had the courage to tell me what I was doing wrong. I confess it has not always been easy listening, and it hurt at times, hurt to the point of tears. But these times were the biggest growth periods in my life. How important it is for us to step back and see ourselves as others see us, both physically and mentally.

One of the persons that I admire most on this earth is my husband. He is the kindest, sweetest person I have ever met; and as hard headed as I am, I am learning to listen to his helpful criticism. The Bible tells us, *Don't refuse to accept criticism: Get all the help you can.* I must stress at this point that you rarely ever hear a critical word come out of his mouth. So when he does have something to tell me, I am learning to listen. Oh, the years it takes us to learn to listen! I would like to suggest that you, too, find someone you very much admire and solicit their help. You might need help with an appearance problem, a personal problem, or a business problem. But don't ask if you are not willing to listen. And make up your mind that you're not going to be hurt by what they say. If you're going to ask for help you *must* be open-minded. Most people when asking for help simply want someone to agree with the decisions they have already made.

I have learned that the most successful people in the world listen twice as much as they talk. Please be advised at this point that you choose the person to whom you listen with care. If success is your goal, then to successful people you must listen. If beauty is your goal, then listen to beautiful people. Even though I am a "talker," I am thankful I had the good sense to listen when someone was offering me an opportunity, and to have the confidence to say, "I think I can do it; I would like to give it a try." Being a part of this wonderful book is just the type of opportunity I'm talking about. When my dear friend, Dottie Walters, asked me to write a chapter, it would have been just as easy to say "no" as it was to say "yes."

Through the years I have had to learn many important lessons. I think one of the most crucial was that I had to accept myself exactly the way I was, I was six feet tall and nothing was going to change that. I wore a size nine shoe, had broad shoulders, hazel eyes, and fair skin. Whether I like these things or not, I cannot change them, so accept them I must! Now don't sit back and say, "Okay, I'm 30 pounds overweight; I will just accept it." I said accept the things about you that you cannot change, like them or not. *Do not* accept the things about yourself you do not like, but that *you can do something about.* I have seen lives almost destroyed by women who refuse to accept a physical characteristic they were born with. If you can't do anything about it, *forget it!* If you can do something about it, *get going!* Why have you waited so long? If I hadn't accepted myself the way I was and made that first speech, I might never have discovered my potential for public speaking. The longer you wait to make that first speech, take that first driving lesson, or lose that first pound, the harder it will get. Make a list of this year's self-improvement projects, and stick to them. You'll love yourself at the end of the year. The Bible tells us you must love yourself before you can love others.

As I Think I Am

Have you ever been able to look at yourself in a mirror and tell yourself how special you are? You are special, you know. How can I be so sure? Because I could look for a thousand years and never find another person exactly like you or exactly like me. That's one of the wonders of this marvelous world. Like your thumb print or snow flakes, there are never two alike. Now from where I sit that makes you a one of a kind original, and the world pays thousands of dollars each day to buy one of a kind originals. If you want to be thought of as special, *think special.* To be special you must care: care how you look, care how you act, care how you dress, put care into everything you do. It is well known you become what you think you are, so think you're special. What have you got to lose?

If right now you are sitting there comparing yourself with one of your friends that you feel can do just about everything, I've got news for you. No one can do everything. We weren't programmed that way. But *everyone can do something.* Thank goodness I realized this many years ago. I thought to myself, "What have I got to lose? If I don't believe in myself and my abilities, then who will?" An amazing transformation began, at that point, to take over my life. The more I acted like I had self-confidence, the more self-confident I became. I found that self-confidence was an act of my own will. The people around me started making comments like, "Well, it's easy for you to speak to 500 people, you have so much self-confidence." Little did they know what was going on in my head. I might be saying to myself, "I'm not sure I can do this," the whole time I was doing it.

As my career grew so did that self-confidence. I took on projects I had never before attempted. I became producer of my own television show, on which I also was the hostess. I made mistakes, sure, but so does everyone. I also did a great deal right. That's the part I choose to remember. A couple of years later I became a regional fashion coordinator for a very large department store chain and loved every minute of it. I will never forget the day I went in to apply for the position. As I look back on it I shudder. For some reason I had the idea that I was probably the only person in town qualified for the position. How I ever got that idea I will never know, but off I went. I walked into the manager's office, gave him my background, and then requested that since I had children, I would like to work the days and hours that I choose. I told him that I would get the job done but to just let me do it the way I wanted. The manager must have liked the approach. I took the position, and started working the following week with a very happy relationship. The day my husband was offered a change for a new adventure in the West Indies I quit with regrets and fanfare, packed up the girls and headed off with him.

Four years ago an opportunity came my way that offered me a chance to truly test my mental capacity. Mine was just one of 150 other applicants for the position. I knew if I was to be considered for this position I must sell myself. Little did I know that I would end up having 16 interviews over a period of four months. I have to admit after interview number twelve, I wondered how long I could go on; but the position required that I be accepted by all the directors of the company, and the challenge of trying to sell myself to that many people intrigued me. After interview number sixteen I was hired as Disneyland's Appearance Coordinator. I now feel I qualify as an expert in the art of interviews! If you have an interview coming up soon, always remember that *you never get a second chance at a first impression,* and that first impression can make or break your chances for a truly terrific job opportunity.

First impressions *are* lasting. Do we judge each other on first impression? You better believe it! Have you met someone new lately? What was your first impression of them? I ask all seminar students to pull from the wonderful memory bank in the brain the vision and feeling they had the first time they saw the car they now own. In almost every case it can be done 100%. Then I ask them to remember the exact vision and feeling they had the 15th time they saw the car. It can't be done! I do this to illustrate just how important first impressions are. They are always the most lasting. Will you meet someone today for the first time? What will your clothes, your hair, your hands, your smile, tell them about you? Will your grooming say this is a person that cares about themselves, this is a person I would like to know better, or would hire for an important position. If they care about themselves, doesn't it add up that they will also care more about a job well done? It has been written over and again how important your grooming and clothes are in an interview, but somehow people just don't catch on because I still hear so much complaining from personnel managers on this subject. When you get dressed and groomed beautifully because you know I am coming to see you, what are you actually saying? You're saying, "I care about you. I respect you. You are important to me and what you *think* is important to me." Thank you. By caring, you have just paid me one of the most sincere compliments I will ever receive. Proper grooming communicates to your employer that you care about him and the company image. Keep in mind, you're not looking at yourself all day, but other people are. Pay them the respect they deserve, give them something beautiful to look at. The position at Disneyland meant that I was responsible for the over-all appearance and image of the 8000 employees, at times not an easy task.

One thing is very clear: when you are thrust into a position of setting a grooming example for 8000 people, you are very careful to choose your clothes with care. For this reason I was always in high heels, even if it meant walking the park for many hours. I found one group of our international visitors just as interested in me as I was in them. As I walked along at six feet three inches, I noticed how the noise level of touring Japanese groups rose. The quiet reserve of these lovely people usually prevented them from asking me to pose for pictures, even though their cameras became very busy. One day, however, as I was walking into the china shop I realized I was being followed by a dear sweet Japanese family. The women, speaking no English, came rushing over to me very excited talking and using sign language. It only took me a moment to realize what I was to do. We all went outside and one by one I would tuck each family member under my arm for their special picture. There was much laughing and excitement as each member took their turn. What a wonderful day that was!

Just as Walt Disney had dreamed of his great magic kingdom over 25 years ago, I also began to dream. My dream was to open a speakers bureau to service conventions coming to Anaheim, and to become well known on the national speaking circuit. It's hard to work at Disneyland and not get caught up in a dream of your own. Walt Disney and his beliefs helped give me courage to act on my own dream.

"Somehow I can't believe there are many heights
that can't be scaled by a man who knows the secret
of making dreams come true. This special secret can
be summarized in four "C's." They are *curiosity,
confidence, courage,* and *consistency,* and the greatest
of these is confidence. When you believe a thing,
believe it all the way. Have confidence in your
ability to do it right, and work hard to do the best
possible job." WALT DISNEY

When I left Disneyland, I held the dual position as
Disneyland Appearance Coordinator, and as the Chair-
man of the Disneyland Speakers Bureau. I gave fashion
seminars, planned motivational programs, and worked
with management on park appearance problems. I wrote
articles for the company paper, and spoke to many conventions and clubs on the Wonderful World of Disneyland.
    Presently, I am President of my own Speakers Bureau.
If I must pinpoint one area of my life that I feel has
contributed most to my success, I would have to say it's my
God-given ability to be a public speaker. My suggestions
to anyone undertaking a difficult task or position: *Have
faith in your ideas and the courage to follow them through.*
Be positive! Never say "I can't"; always say "I'll try." Be
innovative. Create new ideas and ways to improve your
position. Be determined to succeed. Make new friends;
they can really help on "down" days. Listen to suggestions; someone just might have a good idea. *Like* yourself,
and *never* be afraid to tell yourself that you are a pretty
terrific person. Always keep an open mind toward new
opportunities. Be immaculately groomed, keeping in
mind that your body is the temple of God.
    Many people refuse to make an honest judgment of
themselves for fear of what they might have to admit.
They either build illusions or excuses. We all have positive picture-images of types of people, and the way they
look. Let's discuss and imagine a few: The glamorous type,
the tough guy, the girl next door, the business woman, the
wealthy socialite, president of the company. When I men-

tion these types we all get a mental image of how we think they should look, act and dress. Now let's turn this around. When we see people dressed in these manners, do we at once assume that they are wealthy, or the bank president, or successful business woman? Strange as it may seem, *yes* we do. By *your* appearance and your clothes, what are people assuming about you? Selecting becoming clothes is truly a difficult task for many women. No matter how hard they try, they never feel confident with their selection.

Simplicity is a key word in successful dressing. So many women over-do: they over-do accessories, over-do color, over-do prints. Keep it simple and remember, only one star at a time. Your clothes should have beauty in cut, material, and design. Make them fashionable, but inconspicuous. If your friends remember everything you wear and own then something is wrong. The colors are too bright, the print is too bold, the style too shocking; it could be a number of things, but one thing is for sure: you need to take a good long look at your buying habits. Buy clothes that are inconspicuous, and have understated elegance. Make sure that you don't get into the "sameness" rut. Either your own "sameness" rut, such as always wearing the same color, or the group "sameness" rut, where every one looks the same. This is a big mistake made by so many junior and senior high school students. Find your own look, your own identity. Have the courage to be yourself, no matter what the fashion magazines say.

Here are some fashion tips to help you on your way toward your image goal. The first article of clothes that a person sees is the lightest or brightest that you are wearing. Then their eyes go to your feet and travel back up the body. Take a survey and ask yourself which area of the body you would most likely enter into a beauty contest, and which part would most likely be the least. You should now have your first clue as to the areas of the body you will highlight, and those you want to play down. For example, if your hips are a problem area, you would never wear white pants with a dark blouse. When we dress we want to create an optical illusion that makes us look as if we have one of those Vogue Magazine figures, but we must understand our bodies in order to do this. For years I have taught fashion classes and it always surprises me how many women do not, after thirty or forty years, understand what look it is they are trying to achieve. They have never done what I call a body inventory. The shape of the face, its good and bad features, the length of the neck, the shoulders (are they broad? narrow? or in proportion with the rest of the body?). Is the torso high busted, low busted, large busted or no busted? Is the body in proportion with the legs, and are you high or low waisted? I think you get the idea of the type of inventory I mean. How can we dress properly if we do not understand what we are dressing? An interior designer would never think of decorating a room without knowing the good and bad of it (where the windows are and its dimensions). After you have completed your inventory, you should be well on your way to knowing what areas you want to focus on, and what figure problems should be camouflaged.

Many of you have clothes you never wear or don't like. One of the main reasons for this is that you let a salesperson or friend talk you into something.

Questions to Consider Before you Buy

1. *Will the item fit into my basic wardrobe plan?*
   Every woman should have a plan when building a good wardrobe. If she doesn't, five years from now she will still be complainig, "*I have nothing to wear!*" Know your type and stick to it! Know your color plan and stick to it! Start your wardrobe with one basic dress. If you don't have one, get one: a dress that will go everywhere and do everything; a dress that can be dressed up or down. Over the years you will wear that dress more than any other in your closet, so spend a little more and buy a good one. I suggest a suit for your next purchase, always a winner in business.

2. *Are the lines right?*
   Are the lines of the dress best suited to your figure? If you're short, does the dress give a vertical look? Does it give the illusion of more height, or does it cut the figure in half due to a seam or belt?

3. *Is the color right?*
   Color is such an interesting subject. Many people make their livings just telling other people what colors they should wear. In order to know what colors are best on you, take a good long look into the mirror. What color are your teeth, your eyes, your fingernails (unpainted, of course), and your skin? Every human being is born with a color scheme aready decided for him. Do you have yellow, blue, or pink undertones in the skin? If your teeth tend to be very white and your skin fair, you most likely have blue undertones in the skin and your basic color will be black. If your teeth, eyes, and skin have yellow undertone, brown shades would be a good starting place for you. If you have a great deal of pink undertones, then pick navy blue for your basic color. Go to your paint store and pick up one of the marvelous color key charts that shows every color of the rainbow and more with yellow or blue undertones. That is the trick to dressing in the proper color. Wear any color you like but make sure the underlying color of what you wear goes with the underlying color of your skin, teeth, and hair. As much as some people would have you believe how hard it is to pick proper colors for yourself, it isn't! I need only about 15 minutes of your time.

4. *Is the fabric right?*
   The right fabric is also important. The thing to remember here is that certain fabrics add weight to the figure. For instance, you might add 5 to 10 pounds with the wrong tweed suit. Material that shines can do the same thing, so beware.

5. *Is it the proper style for me?*

    Nothing looks much worse than seeing a woman trying to look much younger than her years, or a teenager trying to look much older. Your life style must also be considered here.

6. *Do I have the proper accessories?*

    If you are going to have to purchase all new accessories to wear with the garment, is it worth the price, no matter how much of a bargain it is? Every item in my closet can be worn with a basic color of shoe. I do not like to make my feet the center of attention. Buy a navy blue dress, put yellow shoes with it and I can guarantee no one will miss your feet. Keep in mind you guide my eyes and tell my eyes where to look by the way you accessorize your clothes.

7. *Do I feel comfortable? Is the garment psychologically right for me?*

    No matter how smashing the dress may be on you, it must be in your comfort zone. If the neck line is too low or the slit too high, don't let yourself be talked into it. Once you get it home you will never wear it again.

There is so much more I would like to teach you. I know you want to look as good as you can. No one sets out in the morning to be deliberately poorly dressed or groomed. I truly care about you and want you to have the confidence you deserve.

Write or phone, I would love hearing from you.

Joy de Montaigne
10618 N. 39th Way
Phoenix, AZ 85028
(602) 996-1195

JOY de MONTAIGNE

Joy de Montaigne is a Professional Speaker, Author, Sales Trainer and Consultant. Joy has trained thousands of Salespeople in Non-Verbal Communication - Body Language, Role Playing and Game Playing. Beginning her career over 20 years ago, Joy's studies and research into parapsychology, human behavior, motivation, verbal and non-verbal communication and hypnosis culminated in a 14 year private consulting practice where she trained Salespeople, Public Officials, Administrators and Entertainers in Non-Verbal Communication Techniques. Joy's efforts are now concentrated on Professional Speaking, Seminars on Non-Verbal Communication, Tape Cassette Programs and Writing.

Joy's works include *Stand Up, Speak Out And Win!* a dynamic book on communication which she co-authored with several other top professional speakers, *Closing Encounters Of The Real Estate Kind* - a tape cassette program on Non-Verbal Communication for Real Estate Salespeople and *Individual Dynamics For Women - A Profile For The Dynamic Woman* - a consciousness expansion, self-esteem building tape cassette program for women.

Contact Joy at: Individual Dynamics, P.O. Box 31125, Phoenix, Arizona 85046 (602) 996-1195

People's natures are alike: It is their habits that carry them far apart.
CONFUCIUS

THE PEARL OF GREAT PRICE

by Joy de Montaigne

The Kingdom Of Heaven is likened to a merchant woman seeking goodly pearls, who, when she found one pearl of great price, went and sold all that she had and bought it. On her journey into success, the woman herself is the Pearl Of Great Price. Investing in oneself is a rewarding venture. The rewards are both tangible and intangible. The tangible rewards come packaged in different kinds of material, while the intangible rewards are the greater gifts of the spirit which infuses all material and all life. In order to realize more fully the rewards that await us we must expand our consciousness and build our self-esteem. Distinguishing the various levels of awareness, regarding our Pearls of Potentiality, begins with the four aspects of life: the *Intimate, Home, Social* and *Career.* Each aspect has its own precious jewels. The mind, body, emotions and the psychic faculty house the skills. Body language, role playing and game playing are the tools. The precious jewels are all the people in our world.

Consciousness has its different levels in which all the foregoing work together to maintain the integrity of each level. Should there be flaws in the fabric of consciousness, the skills of the mind, emotions, body and psychic faculty and the tools of body language, role playing and game playing together can remove the flaws and help strengthen the consciousness for more expansion. Our ability to take hold of opportunity when it comes upon the scene of our lives depends upon this expansion. The 12 Basic Non-Verbal Communication Attitudes are the fabric. Woven together they help form a wonderful sustance for communicating our beliefs, opinions and ideas. They are as follows:

1. CONFIDENCE
2. REASSURANCE
3. EXPECTANCY
4. BOREDOM
5. DEFENSIVENESS
6. OPENNESS
7. READINESS
8. SUSPICION
9. SELF-CONTROL
10. NERVOUSNESS
11. EVALUATION
12. FRUSTRATION

Confidence in your ability to confide in yourself and utilize these basic 12 attitudes through self-responsibility gives you confidence-in-action on the many inward levels of consciousness. Self-responsibility puts these attitudes into motion on a positive level of action. The ability to respond to the self positively, strengthens our abilities to respond to others in the same manner. This expands our self-responsibility and produces confidence-in-action on the outward levels of consciousness also.

CONFIDENCE

Reassurance - When an individual has a need for reassurance (as we all do from time to time), and you respond accordingly with confidence, you are helping that individual gain in self-esteem and you build your own self-esteem at the same time.

REASSURANCE

Expectancy can give you a big boost in faith. There is a song entitled "Expect A Miracle". Everyday brings upon the horizon the great expectancy of the miracle, which is the day fulfilling itself. You can expect to add to each day your own miracle - fulfilling yourself. Self-fulfillment is truly the only basis upon which one can give and share. No one can give from an empty vessel.

EXPECTANCY

Boredom cannot be sustained from the moment you become expectant. Boredom is an indication that something new is coming on the horizon. Look up and get ready with great expectancy.

BOREDOM

Defensiveness creates an atmosphere of negativity. Negative control in any situation needs a positive counterpart. Counteracting negative power means converting this negative attitude by using positive attitudes.

DEFENSIVENESS

Openness counteracts defensive behavior. Utilizing the positive attitudes in tending to negative situations brings harmony and balance to the encounters. Should negativity persist without looking for solutions it's time to leave the situation. However, through reasoning together on the basis of positive power, you will win more than you lose.

OPENNESS

Readiness sharpens the senses and hones the skills. Being ready to act in the moment, rather than to react, stimulates the situation and keeps things moving right along. It aides in opening the suspicious mind.

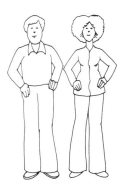

READINESS

Suspicion is a negative attitude. It acts as a warning device in the hands of expanded consciousness. The warning may be directed at another person or toward oneself. In either case, readiness through positive confrontation exposes the suspicion and converts the negative power to positive power through self-control, resulting in positive solutions.

SUSPICION

Self-Control energizes a situation with concentrated effort toward maintaining a positive atmosphere. As others enter your environment and like it they will enjoy being on your ride for a while and also enjoy being away from their own. Self-control puts others at ease. It is a very positive attitude. Self-control is a trust generator.

SELF-CONTROL

Nervousness helps to keep self-control sharp. Self-control puts nervousness at ease. Nervous people can put themselves at ease by exercising self-control and allowing self-confidence to maintain this self-control. This relaxation produces clarity. Clarity and nervousness are not kissing cousins.

NERVOUSNESS

Evaluation is the 11th basic non-verbal communication attitude. Discovering the use of these attitudes to build up or tear down, places you the evaluator in the center of the situation regarding your own decision making processes. Evaluating a situation pulls in as many facts as possible to make a wise decision.

EVALUATION

Frustration can sometimes result from overtaxing the brain. While the mind can continue forever, the brain gets to the point of needing relaxation. Frustration is another negative warning and evaluation finds the best solution for the frustration.

FRUSTRATION

These twelve pearls of non-verbal communication serve humankind along the path of success. Non-verbal communication is the world of Silent Command. When positive and negative power come together in a light bulb, the light goes on. So it is with people. The light is given to everyone who comes into the world! The light within us works on the same principle as seen in electrical lighting. There is the source, the power and the switch. For example, the light of this world is the Sun - Solar Power. This is rapidly becoming a major source of energy for our planet. Humankind's inner Light - Power is also considered a major source of energy for our planet and its inhabitants. It is these lights that continue to lead our world into eras of greater achievement. The switch is our ability to open and close the power lines.

Men and women are the power lines working shoulder to shoulder to build an even better society in which to live. We, our children and our children's children shoulder the responsibilities individually and collectively. We fulfill ourselves through handling our responsibilities effectively, thus, providing ourselves with enjoyment and comfort.

The non-verbal aspects of comfort are many. The rainbow is a vibrant symbol of peace that helps to inspire us to express our non-verbal feelings through color. Textured materials, stylish clothing, homes and automobiles are non-verbal statements. Nature supplies us with the materials for comfort and all this helps to keep us good-natured. Music blends itself into our senses and brings harmony into comfort.

The verbal aspects of communication derive their impetus from the non-verbal realm. Art, science and religion are also avenues through which we express ourselves non-verbally. Through these and many other avenues our *Potentiality* to fulfill our goals is in the future, the *now* and is seen as having been present yesterday. For example, yesterday you had potentiality, today you have it more and tomorrow you shall have even more. *Potentiality* is a dynamic self-perpetuating experience. Once in action, it produces opportunities for our fulfillment. As with color and music, it can be potently in or out of harmony with us. If disharmonious, we know it can be brought into harmony through adjustment, thereby causing the potentiality factor to increase in favor of harmony.

The process of potentiality lives with us every *Now Time!* For instance, it is *Now* 9:00 A.M. *Now* it is 9:00 P.M. No matter what "clock" time it is, we are always in *Now Time.*

We sit on the *ledge* between knowing and unknowing. The feelings we have are expressed *Now* through our *knowledge* of ourselves and our world around us. Unknowing and its potentiality are also expressed. When we become more aware of this process with its potentiality, the unknown becomes more known, creating the way for more knowing.

The ledge where the two meet is a place of adjustment to the unknown becoming the known. For example, when you plan a business event, you *know* that when the guests arrive for the affair, there will be a predominant business air in communications and some social activity will be mixed in. The topics will be primarily business related. During this time, the *home* aspect of your life will be the *unknown* factor. Thoughts will vie for your attention like "I wonder if anyone's home", "Have they eaten", "Did Janie get to her piano appointment on time" etc.

If you succumb to this preoccupation territory, the business affair enters into the unknown realm of awareness for a time and the home aspect takes precedence. When intuition is working in this preoccupation territory, it handles the situation competently by determining the real priorities. It takes action and puts the mind at ease leaving you free to enjoy the business affair. Intuition is a servant which helps to maintain the balance between the world of preoccupation and *Now Time.*

In *Now Time,* many men and women the world over are accepting the responsibilities for caring and tending to the earth's needs and those of its inhabitants. We are in good hands as we share and help one another with our pearls of potentiality we have gleaned from our life experiences, our meditation and prayers. This creates more opportunities for everyone; we reap the benefits together. These benefits are a help to us in our career, social, home and intimate lives. The first benefit is the ability to expand our consciousness regarding the totality of our being. The ability to *be!* Secondly, we are benefited by this same ability that recognizes others in the same light. This creates a climate for open communication.

The third benefit of sharing our pearls is a greater awareness of the true value of these precious gems. This begins with an introduction to the 12 Powers of Life: Imagination, Strength, Order, Wisdom, Freedom, Judgement, Faith, Will, Zeal, Love, Affirmation and Life itself, the culmination of all the value represented. Choose these pearls for they recreate much and cost little. These 12 Powers are the valued pearls given to each of us as a gift when we entered upon the scene of life. *These pearls are forever.*

The first power, imagination, is beautifully revealed in the words of Lord Byron:

> "The beings of the mind are not of clay
> Essentially immortal, they create
> And multiply in us a brighter ray
> And more beloved existence."

Imagination is the light of an idea. An idea is like a pearl, there are no two exactly alike. Their beginnings are very humble and dynamic. The process of maturing an idea works on the same principle as the creating and maturing processes of a pearl. As grains of sand are gathered into the oyster and refined, the sands of time gather into the fertile soil of mind the hopes, dreams and goals of the hopeful and the dreamers. They too are then refined, until one day the dream becomes a reality. Today is reality born of yesterday and grist for tomorrow's mill.

Yesterday, today and tomorrow are three parts in *Now Time,* as are water, ice cube and steam.

Working with the flow of the sea water, the oyster diligently gives of its talents and abilities to bring to the world its finished product. Ideas travel a similar course of endeavor. The merchant woman is an idea whose time has come. She is endowed with these marvelous gifts from her Creator. You and I are the Pearls of Great Price.

When I first began my journey into consciousness expansion techniques 20 years ago, I realized there would have to be the power of *Order* in my life. Confusion would be a hindrance to my being successful. As I set out to bring this order into my personal world, I found many people who offered their love and help. The offering of love and help, and the acceptance of the same, produces infinite capacities when added to and returned again.

These wonderful people are my mate, family, friends, business associates and clientel. They are of my household and I add to it each day. Their love and help I would not do without. In the family of humankind, we take our portion of responsibility for the earth's household upon our shoulders. We each carry what is humanly possible from the tallest man and woman to the smallest child. When I embarked upon my career as a communications counselor, a vehicle to more consciousness expansion, I decided to expand my work to include sales training, professional speaking and writing on non-verbal communication - the world of silent command. This is how and when I discovered my Pearl Of Great Price.

Once *Order* was in place, the powers of *Strength* and *Faith* continually helped me move the mountains necessary for my progress. Then I formed my own company. The Light, the 12 Powers Of Life and the 12 Basic Non-Verbal Communication Attitudes are my foundation. I believe that getting the four aspects of my life into proper perspective (Intimate, Home, Social and Career) was the major personal undertaking in laying this foundation. These aspects are the mortar in my foundation. I have found an inexhaustible source of energy and comfort in these remarkable servants.

The power of *Freedom* is symbolized by the creatures that fly. They fly to live. We live to fly to greater heights of conscious awareness. The symbols of life do not tinkle as sounding brass when love is injected into our understanding. The act of flying is the non-verbal statement that breathes life into the verbal word - flying. Non-verbal statements or acts help us to see word pictures i.e. airplane, hydroplane, trapeze, kites, achievements and success, (She is off and flying).

Self-Esteem, regarding oneself with respect and affection and being worthy of this regard, takes an individual on a flight to higher grounds of consciousness, through the power of righteous *Judgement*. The colors become more vivid and the smiles on the faces of the people are brighter. Life is good and we are *Life*.

The dragon that captures the Pearl Of Great Price can be perceived either as the fire-throwing destructive dragon of yore or our beloved "Puff the Magic Dragon". In any case, we alone *will* determine the outcome of the Pearl and its potentiality.

Business today is a more dynamic happening than ever before. Women are taking to the desks at top executive levels and sharing the common space of business integrity and leadership. Giving to the business world what has been taught at "Mama's knee" is a major growth step for humankind. The majority of people have been taught as children the fundamentals of having the good life with integrity. Men and women have shared this common space intimately, at home and socially as well. Today they work together side by side with *Zeal* and common purposes in the business community. Sharing the financial achievements together, for a job well done, is the core of business integrity and helps keep America strong. We are a team "together we stand—divided we fall". We are the pacesetters for the world. I believe we in this country have individual Self-Esteem that shares itself in the collective Self-Esteem, hence the *United* States Of America. The

Pearls Of Potentiality for this nation are its people - Thank God for us. We are worthy of our message to the world.

Leadership in all areas of living gives life to the Lead-Ship. This spaceship earth is a leader among planets and as we have seen from the moon's perspective, we are a light among the great lights. So too does each individual carry her light. When you greet your mate, your family, friends and your clientel, you literally "light up their lives" and they light up yours. Upon awakening, when morning has broken, we find ourselves in a new day where we light up our own lives too. When we are centered within ourselves and our light, we find stability and security with a sense of strength to carry out our efforts toward achievement. Once the goal of any achievement is realized, we begin again another effort, another event, another experience to fulfill its *won*ders. As a saleswoman, I discovered the *Seven Wonders Of Selling* that help me begin each working day. I share them here with you.

The Seven *Won*ders Of Selling

The selling world, like our planet earth, has its many *won*ders that contribute to the daily success of the salespeople around the globe. I refer to these as the Seven *Won*ders Of Selling. These must be present in every transaction in order for everyone to win. The use of these seven *won*ders provokes effectiveness and efficiency far beyond that already known or anticipated.

The excitement of energizing a sales transaction with the Winner's Attitude produces the Won in *Wonder* and increases our Closings.

1. *Light*
   The first Wonder of Selling is Light, the Light that is given to everyone who comes upon the earth. This

spaceship called earth is propelled through space using the power of Light. We are the recipients of this great inheritance. We professional salespeople walk as eternal lights serving each client in the material sense while also contributing to the consciousness expansion of the societies in which we live. We literally "light up" our clients' lives.

In business, the light of our understanding prepares us for the sales encounters, initiates the communication process, generates leadership and "closes" with confidence.

2. *Service*
"Straight is the way, narrow the gate and few there be that find it". As we walk upon the path of Salesmanship, that many before us have traveled, we reflect upon the lamps they left here to light our way. These lamps were placed by the "way-showers" to provoke in us a burning desire to place our lamps among them in the same spirit of service, for it is after all, service that sparks the third *Won*der of selling.

3. *Power*
In the beginning, we find the word . . . Words are Power expressed verbally. The more positive the attitude behind the word, the more powerful is the word and the more effective is the ability to convert negative power into positive power. Negativity cannot be ignored else it run rampant over the face of the earth. Positive confrontation used in subduing negativity is vital to our well-being when we are involved in transacting business affairs as well as affairs of the social, home and intimate aspects of our lives. Service is the presence of power in Leadership.

4. *Leadership*
Body Power is the key to Leadership. Constructive leadership, as well as destructive leadership, is seen

through Body Power-Non-Verbal Communication. The mental, psychic and emotional faculties determine what Body Power will do — construct or destruct. Professional salespeople who serve their clientele with positive attitudes, motives and positive leadership are the constructive torch-bearers who, with product knowledge, set out to meet the world eye to eye, shaking hands, encountering the negatives and enlightening the clientele.

5. *Motivation*
   A motive for utilizing Seven *Wonders* Of Selling can be positive and/or negative. The concrete results are seen as either having the feet set in cement or the feet put to the pavement. *When we put our feet to the pavement, the world is an open door.* If the feet are set in cement, one is not exactly a pillar in the community. Providing ourselves with positive motives secures success.

6. *Integrity*
   The "nitty gritty" completion of projects and transaction encounters with firmness in purpose and strength of spirit takes unyielding courage. A selling transaction is not unlike deciding to have a family. There are five family circles or aspects that we will consider here. The first family circle is the *Intimate* light that was present on earth before our arrival. Our Mom and Dad fused in an intimate relationship and soon more lights came on the scene. As we entered the earth's atmosphere, we brought with us our own light to help in the lighting process of integrity. Thus enters the second aspect or circle, the *Home*. These two circles have doors so that "we may go in and out and find green pastures", in the *Intimate* and *Home* aspects of our lives. The same is true of professional salespeople and their clientel. When the clientel or customers make a decision to investigate a product, they first come together in a *business* re-

lationship. This constitutes the beginning half of the sales transaction. The other half is, the already presence upon the earth of, the salesperson and product. Integrity is the weaving, product is the material. As the third family group, the *business* family, grows positively, so does integrity. The fourth family aspect is found where all the families meet, in the *Social* realm. This family circle acts as a catalyst for all family life. As we meet our mates, children, parents, friends and business associates in the social circle, we have the opportunity to expand our consciousness and see more clearly the Shining Lamps Of Life.

As we each individually turn inward to contemplate the Light, we enter into the fifth family circle in the Secret Place of the Most High. The family gathers together here, as individuals, with our One Father, and trims the lamps with the oil of love for yet another family reunion.

7. *Completion*
The Seven *Won*ders Of Selling, through to Completion, are the dynamite behind the Professional Salesperson. As dynamite can destroy a hillside just for the sake of destruction, so too can it be used to clear the way for a more meaningful structure. The Seven *Won*ders Of Selling can be used to *Build A Better You as you catch your Pearl Of Potentiality to grow a healthy, wealthy, loving family circle.* The Pyramid of Selling has a cornerstone. *You* Are It! *Sell! Sell! Sell!*

Faith in these Seven *Won*ders and their application has inspired me to new heights that before, I saw only in my dreams. Now my dreams have become realities. On my journey to here, I have found, as stated by Feltham, "Works without faith are like a fish without water, it wants the element it should live in. A building without a basis cannot stand; faith is the foundation, and every good action is as a stone laid". We have the inherent capabilities to do anything we conceive. The Pearl Of Potentiality remains latent within if Faith does not spark the actuality of doing, giving and serving from the heart of the Pearl Of Great Price.

Today as you carry forward your yesterday's experience to guide you into your tomorrows, remember that *Now Time* is the only reality. It is in each *Now Time* where success is found. I wish you the very best that success has for you. Your Pearls await you in the fertile soil of mind and one by one your dreams become realities. Dream the big dream for you and your household. Nourish your inner servants that attend your every need. *Give* to the world from your Pearls - *Receive* - and *Give* again.

THE FLAME

The family of man and the family of woman are as one and yet . . . not the same.
We are the torchbearers, the Lights of Life who carry our individual flame.
We know the oneness and share in its might,
And we are careful in trimming these lamps of Light.
Our body and Soul move together as one,
And our Lights shine as brightly as our Eternal Sun.

Joy

Pansy Ellen Essman
110 Component Dr.
San Jose, CA 95131
(408) 263-9861

PANSY ELLEN ESSMAN

Pansy spent her first 20 years on a farm in North Dakota. During the war years she was an aircraft electrician and for 20 years she worked in the electronic industry. She is the mother of two daughters and grandmother of three.

At age 55 she left her job to build a very successful manufacturing company because she chose to catch the dragons' pearls and string them on her string of knowledge.

Receiving two national awards in 1976 for her accomplishment, Pansy now has the distinction of being the first person to change the way babies have been bathed for 200 years. Pansy was named Business Woman of the Year by ICSB, International Council of Small Businesses.

"To See Things in The Germ: This is Genius."
LAO-TSZE

"YOU ARE NEVER TOO OLD TO CATCH THE DRAGON'S PEARLS."

by Pansy Ellen Essman

When the Dragon threw his pearls I reached out and caught them! The Pearl of imagination, intuition and a positive mental attitude. With these three Pearls I was able to turn a dream into reality in spite of educational background or age, for I was 52 years young at the time.

My dream was inspired by my first granddaughter who was most difficult to bathe and I really didn't know why. In my dream I was bathing little Letha in this beautiful sponge bath aid that looked like a cushion with a cavity cut in it, the shape of the baby's body. It cradled Letha in secure comfort. She was cooing, laughing and enjoying her bath. I realized it was a dream, and when I awoke the image of the bath aid stayed with me for months. In a very haunting way I kept seeing the bath aid in my mind's eye. Here was a Pearl in my hand that could benefit all mankind and I knew I had to do something with it.

The Search

I went in search of the polyurethane sponge I saw in my dream. It was months before I found the information at the telephone company's "out of state" yellow pages. I chose a company in Edgewater, New Jersey that made the kind of sponge material I needed. I placed my order for several blocks and waited excitedly for their arrival. After receiving the blocks I would sit and look at them and wonder how I could cut the cavity in the soft sponge. I kept asking myself how? - how? can it be done? I took the Pearl of imagination and let it work for me far into the night. I knew there had to be a way to cut this cavity because I had seen the finished product in my dream. Soon my subconscious took up the problem and the images started flowing —and there it was—a simple easy way to do the cutting. Overjoyed in receiving another Pearl I went to work designing the cutting equipment that was needed.

My years on the farm in North Dakota, those spent being an aircraft electrician during the war and the knowledge gained in the electronic industry were to prepare me for the Pearls of knowledge I was to receive in mechanics which enabled me to understand and build the machinery I needed.

When we reach out and catch the Pearls of imagination, intuition and wisdom we make them our own by stringing the Pearls on our own string of knowledge and keep them alive with a positive mental attitude.

Hang On!

Keep adding Pearls to your string as often as possible and never let anyone remove them by their negative attitude. Oh, they will try many times over to remove your Pearls from the string only to replace them with false beads of fear and doubt which so easily alters self-esteem. When our self-esteem is diminished with fear and doubt we do less, we don't believe that we can do more. Whenever anyone tells me "it can't be done" that is when I look for a way to do it. I learned to listen for only the positive and informative part of my encounters with the people who pass my way. There is something we can learn from every person who passes our way, even the unimaginative. They also have their Pearls to pass on if you are ready to receive them. Enjoy your achievements as well as your endeavors. They are yours and don't let anyone make them less than they are. Neither age or education should have a bearing on whether or not to step up front and say, "I will do it."

Courage of a Dragon!

It was at age 55 that I left a full-time job to start my own manufacturing business. With only an eighth grade education I knew the odds against me were great and to make it would take the courage of a dragon. It was friends, relatives and co-workers who laughed at me when I decided to leave my job and start manufacturing the infant bath aid. I was soon to learn that I had few friends, and not one of them thought I would be able to handle my new venture. Having an undying conviction that all mothers the world over needed such a bath aid and that I alone knew how to manufacture it, I couldn't keep it from them. I had to do what I could, no matter how hard it might be. Once you have knowledge never let it pass by you or it will be lost forever.

I prepared myself to do all I could for the chance to use and enjoy all the Pearls on my string and reached out to catch even more whenever the dragon came to the shore and threw them. I studied from the books that aided me in marketing, advertising, financing and administration. I learned from everyone who passed my way and I exchanged Pearls of knowledge with them. I vowed never to stop learning and thereby diverted possible failures. Failures are only learning curves after all.

I had finished building the machinery and bought a small supply of urethane sponge for the bath aid. I cleaned out a little chicken coop that set on my mother's property and with her encouragement I worked long hours cutting and packaging the bath aid. I shipped them to retail stores located in a 60 mile radius from the shop, knowing that one day I would have to reach the national market place. That would mean more material, a larger building, representatives, advertising and a lot more money.

I thought then that selling my company was the only way to get the bath aid to the market place fast; however, I was wrong. The companies I showed the bath aid to were hesitant, not sure that it would sell, so they turned it down. I was still sure it would be the best bathing aid on the market, and it looked like I would be the one to put it there.

It was my sisters and brother who came to my aid and loaned me $35,000. I'm sure at this point they never expected to see their money again.

Enter The Marketplace

I put the money to good use. I rented a 5,000 sq. ft. building and set the wheels turning. I joined the Juvenile Manufacturing Association and participated in a trade show in New York. It was there that I gathered more Pearls for my string and learned what a trade show was all about. It was at this first show that the representatives for other companies asked to represent my products in the market place. Just what I hoped would happen—and it did!

Letting go of fear and doubt enabled me to move along faster on the road to success, fulfilling my hopes and dreams. Dreams of helping mothers to bathe their babies more easily, keeping them securely comfortable and happy. I hoped that one day I could contribute something for all mankind—and now I have.

Chosen in 1976 for two awards, one from I.C.S.B. as Business Woman of the Year for my accomplishments in boot-strapping my venture into a million dollar business, and the second for New Product Idea of the Year from my customers—the Retail Association, N.I.N.F.R.A.

So often when you've achieved success you will hear people around you say, "You're so lucky." I wonder if it was luck at all, and yet it could be. Are you "lucky" when you catch the dragon's Pearls? Are you "lucky" when you learn from other's experiences? Are you "lucky" when you decide to take a chance and put everything you have on the line? Are you "lucky" because you worked long hours each day, believing in what you were doing, accepting disappointments with courage and never letting go of a positive attitude? If it is luck, then I've become a Lucky Success in my senior years. Those companies who now imitate me are proof that I have arrived and attained my goal of "Lucky Success" in a rain of pearls.

Susan Hay
3334 Blue Ridge Court
Westlake Village, CA 91361
(805) 496-1035

SUSAN HAY

Sue Hay came to Dynique from Australia a mere five years ago and we shall always be grateful to her native land for directing this genuinely warm, loving and success-oriented woman to our shores. Sue often repeats the story of her journey from the time when things looked hopelessly destitute to her present success. She does this not as a braggart expounding on how she did it on her own, but as a means to show the people whose lives she touches in her work that they too can dare to dream of, and achieve success. She is quick to point out that the only limits are those that are fixed in your own mind. Sue's words come directly from her experience. When she first began in Australia, all those same "blocks" were milling through her mind as she walked from door to door selling her supplies of soap products. The familiar lament of "I have no education, no money and no hope" rang in her ears as she cleaned patches of other women's ovens in the never-ending demonstration of her wares. But, she had persistance and a belief in herself and that alone helped her to never give up and always seek a way to improve her situation.

The tides of success began coming in as she and her husband, Col, and baby, Lisa, arrived in America and she began her career in Dynique. Once again, she started at the bottom, but using Dynique as a vehicle to achieve her goals, before long Sue's dreams began to take the shape of reality and she steadily moved upward in her chosen profession.

Today, Sue Hay has many achievements to her credit. As Director of Training she has taken all her knowledge of positive motivation, added the lessons she learned through her own experiences and shaped them into a viable and comprehensive sales training program which is taught to thousands of distributors each month across the nation. Additionally, Sue keeps a watchful eye on the fashion industry and is responsible for helping in the creation of new products that fill the needs of today's woman. Coupled with this is her development of easy-to-follow procedures in the use of those products.

Sue Hay's time is in constant demand and, like all truly successful people, she finds the time to spend with all those who need her. Success has not changed Sue in her attitudes about people and her responsibilities to them. Above all else, she teaches that Dynique is a "people business" and Sue Hay has built her success not on the want of money, prestige or power, but on a genuine caring for people and a desire to help them create their own success.

Adversity is imagined as a Darkening of the Light but should be regarded as an opportunity for growth. When yielded to as wholly negative, one will be defeated by despair. Accepted as a catalyst that can awaken new avenues of regeneration, adversity becomes the harbinger of Deliverance.
TAO

THE LAND OF OPPORTUNITY

by Susan Hay

Just a few days ago, I raced into our garage . . . and stopped dead in my tracks. The smell of leather was overwhelming—and it was emanating from our new two-tone brown and beige *beautiful* Rolls Royce. My husband, Colin, and I had talked of plans to purchase the prestigious Rolls for "image value" within our business. Together with our business associate, we set a goal for the realization of this dream. Just over a month ago, the goal was achieved . . . And two Rolls Royces were purchased. One, for our friend and his family . . . and one for us.

I couldn't help but reflect back to the first car we had owned on American soil. The upholstery was unmistakably vinyl, covered with tattered two-tone plastic. The car was an old blue Chevrolet and had cost us $500.00.

It was almost Christmas, 1974 . . . and we had just arrived in America. I remember, we looked at the car, then at each other . . . A rather dubious Christmas present!

Col and I had decided to leave our country, Australia, and try our luck in America . . . the land of Opportunity!

At that time, all we had was a very strong determination *not* to have to go back home as "failures."

Through an acquaintance, we became involved in the exercise business. We impulsively invested in a franchise for the State of Florida, for the right to market an "in-home" exercise unit. So we flew to Miami early December.

Our first week was spent finding a place to live, an office and a full-time babysitter for our eleven-month-old daughter, Lisa. By the time all that was accomplished, there wasn't too much left-over for a car.

The weeks before Christmas were very busy for us as we rushed here and there, trying to establish a new life, a new business . . . and fight a strong feeling of isolation.

That Christmas, we didn't have the heart, or the time, to buy a Christmas tree. So our first American Christmas was rather lonely and miserable in hot, damp Miami. But we did have each other, and we made a promise, that each Christmas would be progressively better, that December 25th, 1974.

From somewhere in the midst of our luggage, we dug out a poem entitled: "Don't Quit." It always had a special meaning for us in happier days, and this time we clung to each word as though it was a comforting friend:

DON'T QUIT

When things go wrong, as they
   sometimes will,
When the road you're trudging
   seems all up hill,
When the funds are low and the
   debts are high
And you want to smile, but you
   have to sigh,
When care is pressing you down
   a bit,

Rest if you must, but don't you
quit.

Life is queer with its twists and
turns
As every one of us sometimes
learns,
And many a failure turns about
When he might have won had
he stuck it out.
Don't give up though the pace
seems slow,
You may succeed with another
blow.

Often the goal is nearer than
It seems to a faint and faltering
man
Often the struggler has given up
When he might have captured
the victor's cup.
And he learned too late, when
the night slipped down,
How close he was to the golden
crown.

Success is failure turned inside
out—
The silver tint of the clouds of
doubt.
And you can never tell how close
you are,
It may be near when it seems
afar;
So stick to the fight when you're
hardest hit—
It's when things seem worst that
you mustn't quit.
                    —Selected.

Unfortunately, our exercise business was not a success.
We were fighting what amounted to overwhelming odds.
Our product was sold through T.V. advertising, and the

cost of T.V. leads was crippling. Because the product retailed for approximately $400.00, we needed financing. Which brought us to our biggest problem. We were not only from "out of town" . . . but we were also "foreign out-of-towners" and loan companies were not interested in talking to us.

Both Col and I had worked full-time twelve hours a day for nearly eighteen months . . . and we had serious problems.

Col has always been a man I love, respect and greatly admire. When we met, he was a self-made man on his way up in the world. He had worked his way from sales distributor to president of a direct sales company in Australia . . . within *two years*.

Then, in a few short weeks, his whole world was turned upside-down. External pressures had been brought to bear which literally forced the company out of business. He had immediately flown to America to try and save the company, but it was already too late.

Now, when I happened to catch the desperate look on his face, it was more than I could bear. I would have to fight a feeling of total panic as I contemplated the consequences of another serious set-back.

And then . . . just as our poem promised . . . "the silver tint in the cloud of doubt."

By a series of very fortunate events, we were introduced to the incredible skin care product that we market, very successfully, today. Once again, the words in the poem had come true for us. If we had "quit" our exercise business, we would never have been "in the right place at the right time" to be introduced to our success.

Of course, our beginnings in Dynique were not easy either. *Nothing worthwhile is ever easy*. We started with me as a "guinea pig" for our skin care product. Within four weeks I was completely thrilled and excited with the results of our Aloe Vera based product. I couldn't wait to get out and start showing it to other ladies.

So I was given the job of "test-marketing" the product, through the Direct Marketing system. We believe this to be the fairest and most profitable system for all concerned, going directly to the consumer.

I established my customers by setting up appointments on the telephone from home. I used a cross-index directory and started in our neighborhood. I discovered the truth that *"strangers are simply friends we haven't met yet,"* and gradually built up a flourishing retail business.

My objective had been to "sell" my husband on getting involved one hundred percent. I knew, from past experience, that when he directed the force of his incredible drive into a *good* and worthwhile idea, the result would be outstanding success.

So, once again we became a team and put all of our energies into creating a business based on this product. Naturally, there were some set-backs and obstacles to overcome, but we had such faith and belief in our product . . . it seemed impossible to fail.

About that time we formed a business alliance with a man who was to become a dear and close friend. Fred Pape greatly enriched our Dynique World with his own inimitable brand of charm and charisma, along with an extensive knowledge of the cosmetic industry. Guided by Fred's background and expertise, we took our first steps into the World of Cosmetics as a close-knit, supportive team.

Through Fred, we've had the opportunity to learn, first-hand, the value of teamwork operating through the Master-mind principle: (This well known success principle refers to the combination of two or three minds working together with a common interest or goal . . . this creates an even more powerful *Master-mind,* capable of a much higher level of thought, intelligence and creativity.)

The introduction of cosmetics into our lives was an important turning point in our journey to success. We always had many requests for cosmetics from customers who were thrilled with the skin care products. This reinforced our belief in the Direct Marketing system and emphasized the need for us to expand our service with products that complemented our line.

Then Fred developed a seminar workshop for Corrective and Creative cosmetic training ... a service greatly needed and appreciated by ladies, young and old. He developed this great idea a step further by writing a book, entitled "Dynique's Lovely Illusions," based on his wealth of cosmetic knowledge and experience. And this book is used as the basis of our cosmetic training today.

Our lead skin care product is a natural, Aloe Vera based Contour Lift treatment. Every day we see evidence of how this really helps people, not only by helping to rejuvenate the skin, but also with acne problems. This has never failed to give us renewed faith and belief that we are doing the right thing. *It always seemed too good to be true, that we had found a way to help people and make money at the same time.* But we remembered an important message: *"Money is merely the measuring stick of the quality and quantity of service you render to other people."* And, we discovered that we were *truly in love with our work.*

This feeling has not changed over the past few years ... although the job description has altered quite considerably.

I will never forget the night that Col was appointed President of Dynique ... *two years* after we started as distributors. It still gives me chills when I think of it ... and realize the importance of "Don't Quit!" You always have another chance.

My job description is a little different, too. I have several other titles besides Loving Wife. They are Director of Training, Director of Retail Development and Proud New Mother of Christine Susan, aged seven months.

Over the past few years our wealth has increased immeasurably, and I'm not referring to money. *The true wealth lies in the "people experiences" we've had since living in America. We think of it as being "people wealthy."*

The people that have touched our lives, since Dynique, have come from all walks of life. We've been in the fortunate position of being able to *help people overcome their self-imposed barriers to success.* Helping them recognize their true potential through our training classes, then helping them apply this newfound potential and creativity to something they can believe in.

This is only because we are part of a business concept that represents Free Enterprise, or earning what you are worth. And this is the birthright of *everyone* born in a free country, like America.

Needless to say, we now work with literally thousands of very fine Americans. Some of the people who have become part of our Dynique Family have come through terrible adversity to outstanding success. Their stories are heart-rending . . . and beautiful, because they are actively creating their own happy ending.

Recently, I read an incredible book, "Never Underestimate the Selling Power of a Woman" by Dottie Walters, an author I greatly respect. Something she said in her book really caught my attention . . . "To be successful, you must *love* what you do."

We feel that is an important key to our success. It is an exhilarating, exciting experience to be achieving new and greater sales records together with a team of people who all . . . *love* what they are doing.

It is my belief that there are other definite reasons for our success in what amounts to a short period of time. These reasons are very *important ingredients in any recipe for success.* They are *attitude* and *belief,* working hand in hand with the *law of cause and effect.*

In other words, you must have a great *attitude* about yourself, your abilities and your product. You must *believe* totally in what you are doing. *believe* sincerely that you are doing your best to help people through your product and service.

Then you must carry this a step further by living in harmony with the *law of cause and effect,* or "What you hand out comes back." So, if you have been "handing out" or projecting gloom, pessimism, negativity, unpaid bills, etc. . . . guess what you have in your life!

But the Law also says that if you approach each customer with a sincere desire to help her and find her specific needs, and fill her life with happiness and sunshine . . . then wealth, success and happiness will return to you.

This is the message that we expand on in our Training Schools. And every person who comes in *ready to listen* can help make their part of the World a little bit better.

Guard Your Words:

Another very important aspect of the Law of Cause and Effect is the power of words. Words can be wonderful, comforting friends . . . or bitter, destructive, hateful enemies . . . depending on how you choose and use them. It is important to realize that words are actually *things*.

I have always been aware of their power. As a child, I loved studying English because there were so many wonderful new words to learn. Once I was labeled "pretentious" by a teacher because I was "showing off" using too many "big" words. I remember how hurt I was . . . I didn't even know what half of my words meant. I just loved the wonderful, magical sounds they created. But, I did learn a new word from the experience!

When we understand the psychology of a sales presentation, we realize the importance of painting "word pictures" for our customers, so they can appreciate the value of our product. But, on a deeper level, we are all the sum total of our thoughts (words). So be sure you harness this awesome power and . . . *guard your words*. Then ask your good "word friends" . . . love, peace, harmony, empathy, success, health, friendship and happiness . . . to become a part of your life, so you can share them with others.

As I look back on the events of the last few years, it all seems a little hard to believe. It certainly is a story of a nightmare turning into a beautiful dream, for us and many others.

We need to remember, with gratitude, America is truly the Land of Opportunity . . . for Opportunists. Where else could such a dream come true!!

Roseanna Cary
1636 Lynden
So. Pasadena, CA 91030
(213) 799-5725

ROSEANNA CARY

A native Californian, Roseanna Cary is a Professional Salesperson, and First Vice President of "Women in Management." She is a recognized speaker to corporations, professional associations and business groups, a professional marketing person who uses expertise to design and promote major marketing programs, and sell products to industrial retail and consumer buyers.

She has been a keystone speaker at business seminars and career planning workshops. Her speeches have sold to radio stations around the country.

Some of her speeches have included subjects such as:

Creative sales as a career.
Rewards in creative sales
Successful Women . . . You Can Be One Too.
Success—Professionalism in Your Career.

Roseanna, the mother of four children is working on her Masters of Business Administration at California Western University.

All matter can be changed into energy. All energy can be changed into matter. Neither becomes totally the other. Nothing is ever totally destroyed. When what is created completes itself in exhaustion, it returns to its source hidden in the non-manifested. From within the non-manifested things begin to manifest anew.
TAO

"SUCCESSFUL WOMEN: YOU CAN BE ONE TOO"

by Roseanna Cary

Little did I know when I was chosen to take a special course in Sales, open to a very selected few, that I would be faced with the shock of my life before it would even start.

The Personnel Manager at the Optical Company I worked for informed me of a wonderful seminar the Urban League and Avery International were giving in Professional Selling Techniques. This course would be open for twenty minorities (Women were one!) who had worked in the sales field, but who needed more background in direct sales techniques.

As I needed more background and mobility to achieve my goal and get into outside sales, I applied for the seminar, but I truly held little hope I would be selected. Of the several hundred applications, twenty were chosen. We would work from seven to ten, five nights a week, and on Saturday for a scheduled two weeks. Mr. Dick Kling,

Director of Training for Avery International, was to teach the course. This course was to be the same course Avery's sales people receive after they have sold Avery products for one year. The classroom training would last for three weeks, and involve a trip to San Diego to see the actual Avery Personnel receiving the same instruction we would receive as we sat in on the class Mr. Kling was giving there.

Participating in this class was a *very major turning point in my career* and was a very exciting opportunity to learn and use the offered knowledge in an outside sales job.

How Could I Go On?

It was a busy Christmas Season. Our family is a happy one. We had four beautiful children, two girls and two boys. Cynthia was our high school student who loved animals and constantly complained her school library did not have enough books on that subject. She had read everything she could find on animals. She had applied and been accepted at Cal Tech College, and planned to go on to Davis Veterinarian School in California. She was in a whirl of Christmas parties when she complained of pain in her stomach. When we took her to the doctor, he said, "It is Hepatitis, but don't worry, people do not die of it anymore. No doubt something she ate at one of the parties." Three of her classmates came down with it, and all of them had to be immunized.

But Cynthia sank lower and lower. The doctor was weeping as he told us, "She is gone. She had no natural immunity. Sometime in her life, when she met that disease, it was lying in wait for her."

We were all racked with grief. How could I go on with my life? Years ago a friend gave me a copy of the Alcoholics Anonymous creed when I had to cope with that problem in a dear relative. It came back to me now in this time of deep pain.

"God grant me the Serenity to accept the things I cannot change, the Courage to Change the things I can, and the Wisdom to know the difference."

REINHOLD NIEBUHR

Should I go on with the Avery Sales Course, even tho my eyes and heart were filled with tears. Work is a blessing. It was something tough to hold onto . . . to throw my whole self into. My family said "Yes, Go carry on."

Then we had an inspiration. We asked our many friends and relatives not to send flowers to the funeral. But to give money instead to a special trust fund. The fund buys animal books for our South Pasadena High School. They put a plaque in the school library honoring our little girl, and somehow the thought that together we were helping other children who had a dream of healing animals helped all of us.

The Wisdom To Know

The selling class was very hard as I was understandably very emotionally upset. In the first ten minutes we introduced ourselves by giving our name, family background, and occupation to the class. When my time came to say how many children we had I didn't know how to handle the question and started to say four, but didn't want the class to know of my daughter's death. In my hesitation I became very upset, but I remembered the Serenity Prayer and dried my tears. I would go on!

The days progressed very rapidly and the course was very intense. This helped to keep my mind off our loss and was the best therapy. The course required each of us involved to present a product and sell it to the instructor. These presentations were all recorded on video tape for critiquing later by the students. We had to be able to sell the product to high management in any company setting. This was very difficult to do, as we had never been exposed to this type of selling. Those who finished had a great sense of confidence and accomplishment. The course was my salvation emotionally and in my career.

The Courage To Change

Next, my husband and I made the decision for me to leave the Optical Company and begin to explore which field would give me the best and fastest training and experience. After several exploratory interviews and talking with management recruiters we felt I should go into Business Machine Sales, as this is one of the most competitive fields in sales. We were informed by many knowledgeable people that the most difficult part of outside sales was "cold selling" and "canvassing" which selling business machines requires. Also many large companies offered extensive training courses in sales as well as products. Even armed with the Avery course I still felt I definitely needed heavy training. I went to work for Pitney Bowes in April 1977 as a sales representative.

The business machine field at that time was dominated by men. It offered a real challenge for a woman. I had a difficult time at first, especially with the technical parts of the product. I was sent to Philadelphia for two weeks in September for an intensive training program (which included the respected Xerox Professional Selling Skills Course, which reinforces the ability to make sales presentations). I was able to finish the course in a three way tie with two other class mates (both men) and number one among the western region students.

After completing the course, I was first in sales for Pitney Bowes for three months running. I finished the year as a Sales Leader in the top five percent of the company's nationwide representatives, never dropping below the third top sales representative in our office. As a result I won a trip to the Sales Leader Conference in Puerto Rico. I kept the Serenity Prayer in the front of my appointment book.

The selling skills I learned during my one and one-half years with Pitney Bowes were invaluable. The training required book work and field training. Probably the most important asset it gave me was the confidence I was lacking. I wanted to share my new knowledge and began giving speeches to professional groups. The presentations led to a workshop at the Career Planning Centers Annual Convention (over 10,000 people attended). My workshop had standing room only and was so successful that I was asked to give it twice, which again had a standing room only crowd. How far I had come from the Toy Party Lady who quit because she could not cope.

Twelve Good Ideas

I would like to share with you some of the things I have learned as a Professional Salesperson:

1. *Take chances:* In order to have success you must take risks. Don't be afraid to move up.

2. *Watch your appearance:* When I started with Pitney Bowes, I needed to learn to cope with problems peculiar to women: How to carry a purse and briefcase without looking loaded down and lopsided. This was solved by a small purse available in stationery stores called a mini briefcase, just big enough to hold calculator business cards, pens, comb, keys and kleenex. This fits under your arm and looks professional.

   It is very important to dress professionally. From the very onset of a sales call your appearance says: "I am serious, I am a professional, and I am here to serve." You must overcome the objections of the customers thinking of you as "Just a woman," and have them think of you as a Salesperson, who is professionally trained to help solve their business problems.

3. *The lunch-tab problem:* Another problem many women in sales run into is picking up customers' lunch bills gracefully. Many men can be easily offended by women paying their lunch bill, but this is something you must do to maintain a professional status. I found that credit cards are the least offensive way to handle this. I picked out several restaurants in my sales area and became known to them. I would go in early and tell them I would be

paying, and to bring the bill to me. After a few such occasions these restaurants became very helpful in tactfully putting the bill near me, therefore, overcoming the question of who was paying.

4. *Coping with the "Wolf Man" Problem:* I also ran into the common problem which most women in sales do, that of the male sexual advances. When I started, I almost expected passes from my customers which were small owner/manager businesses. And finally it happened. I overcame the problem by first ignoring the suggestions as if I did not hear or understand. This usually works. If a second advance was made, I would say firmly that "I was in no way interested, and was here to talk business." This answer let the customer know where I stood. My customers respect me. They like to buy a machine from a dedicated professional.

5. *Be Visible: Be available for all jobs:* Never say, "That's not my job!" Do something new *gladly* and learn from it.

6. *Look at other positions in your company while working in your current job:* When there is an opening, ask for the position, don't wait for it to be offered to you as that rarely happens. No one knows what you are thinking!

7. *Use professional business organizations for support, training and exposure:* There are many organizations geared for women that give backup and support for all types of career potentials.

8. *Remember—Women are good in sales:* They are organized, thorough and follow up very well. Women have an advantage in sales because they do not threaten a male client's personal area. Women are able to talk easier with men. Most men do not think of women as a threat, and therefore can be sold easily.

To get into sales a woman must be organized, motivated, and able to get out on her own. In sales you do
not punch a time clock, no one knows where you are
at a given time; sales results tell the story of how
much time you are working. Sales give you an unlimited income based on how much time and concen-
tration you are willing to put into your work. Women
tend to do a more thorough job due to their nature.
Inner feelings convince them that if they don't, they
won't be able to compete with men. And for this same
reason women do follow up. In most sales interviews
that are conducted by salesmen across a desk, there
is a barrier. If a salesman walked around the desk to
show his presentation or put an agreement down in
front of a client for signature, the client might feel
threatened. Women can sit near a client on his side of
the desk to make a presentation or present an agreement for signature without the client feeling
threatened.

9. *Achieve a Positive Self-Image:* In sales, self-image is
very important. The ability to take NO for an answer
and not take it personally is difficult. You hear many
more NOes in sales than you hear YESes. Many
sales people take Noes personally, and become need-
lessly discouraged. This reflects in their performance, and their earnings. No one sells every client,
one sale in five presentations is the national average.
Remember these odds.

The ability to project your self-image is important
and high self-esteem or ego is important. A woman
may not feel this self-esteem at first. However, it will
come as she succeeds and the more this confident
feeling comes, the more success she will enjoy. Always think positively, call on five to sell one.

10. *Do some Networking:* This is a large part of the value
of women's organizations. Networking helps overcome burdens women find in the business world. By

helping other women, you will grow, and find they will help you in return.

11. *The Future is here:* Sales have a good growth potential for women: A recent article in the November 24, 1978 Pasadena Star News reports. "The areas of business that offer greatest growth for women are marketing, sales, finance and production."

12. *My 10 "secrets" for getting ahead in Sales are:*

Get Started at any level you can find a job.
Learn more at every opportunity
Don't be discouraged by "no."
Realize that being a woman is an asset.
Watch for chances to move up the ladder.
Ask for a better job, don't be shy.
Put your whole heart into your work.
Rise above personal problems.
Join organizations that will give you support.
Look professional and act professional.

How I Learned To Cope

I have given many speeches to women's groups. One of my favorite topics is "Successful Women: You Can Be One Too!" I was 35 years old before I realized that I had the potential of becoming a "Successful" woman. I was born in the Los Angeles area to a middle class family. I was the oldest of four children. My mother spent much loving time with us and my father contributed greatly to my future. He owned his own business and was a strict disciplinarian yet he was fair. This trait helps me most in a business environment. (All their children are successful in their careers.)

When I was growing up it was not expected that girls would do anything but become wives and mothers. Therefore all my early training at home was toward that end: cooking, sewing and house cleaning. I was married on my seventeenth birthday and finished my senior year of high school pregnant with my first child. That first summer of marriage I worked in an accounting firm as a file clerk and typist, and though I enjoyed it and learned a lot I never took working seriously. For the next fourteen years I raised my children, was a housewife and stayed home, which was what was expected of me and all I expected of myself. During this period of my life I felt an urge to go to work. Many of my friends worked and kept saying how much they enjoyed being out in the public, being creative and having money to spend on things they couldn't afford on their husband's check. But my husband was making better money than most of our friends combined incomes and he was against my working. I did make a few attempts at earning some extra money. I sold toys on a party plan and I did very well in the sales part but the time it took delivering and sorting orders had my husband upset, so I quit. I didn't understand how to balance work and family. I was overwhelmed.

Trying Times

At the age of twenty-three my husband started his own business. We sold a small rental home we had to provide the cash for this venture. When our last child was born I became seriously ill with meningitis. We were not allowed to leave the house, even food was brought to us. For three months we lived this way. I couldn't even get out of bed without help. My husband refers to this time of our marriage as the second time we were broke. The first was when we were married: we didn't have anything but my husband's income as a box boy, which was meager! When I was able to get around, my husband wanted me to work and help with his business. Even though I was still in traction, I was his typist. While doing this I did not feel I made any real achievement, but it was my "woman's duty" to do the typing. This business lasted about a year until my husband was enticed back into a full time job. So I then stayed home again and raised our children.

But I Yearned To Do Something Creative

On the day I took my youngest child to start Kindergarten, I applied for a job at Sears Roebuck. After a background of fourteen years with no work I was lucky to be hired for a job in catalog telephone sales. I was afraid of the job, knowing that my husband would have a fit if I wasn't at home when our children were home. Then I had an idea. To my surprise it worked! I was hired after explaining to Sears that my hours would have to be 9:00 to 2:00! The emotions I had knowing I was going to work are indescribable. To do something to relieve the feeling of frustration I was feeling at home was terrific. My husband happily agreed that I could work those hours. I stayed with Sears for two years, moved very rapidly in the company and never deviated from my 9:00 to 2:00 hours. I then moved to the Main West Coast Headquarters which was the show place of all Sears management. I concentrated on the few hours I had.

More Problems

At that time my husband went back into business for himself, and I felt I needed to help him again. I left Sears and helped him as his office manager.

The business was doing very well, until one of our clients lost a customer that provided seventy-five percent of their business. They then hired us to get the contracts into our client's name. In return for this work, in lieu of cash, they offered us stock. We ended up owning sixty percent of the company and running it. The previous management had alienated the prime customer so badly that we ran out of money before the attorneys could straighten the mess out. We had to close the company. While we were trying to make it work, we ran short of cash and my husband again had to work for someone else. We had sold some of our investment properties and had even poured that money into the business. We were broke again for our third time. As money got tighter I decided that I would go out and earn money, for food and insurance, by working for another company. I had learned much about business and about coping with family and work.

Start At The Bottom

I applied at large optical firm in Pasadena for any entrance level job they had. I felt that I knew a lot but I couldn't find the words to put down on on the application. At that time the only job they had was a receiving clerk. *I knew that I could make any job that I wanted important and a springboard to better things.* This was a company with growth. I think it is very important to consider growth in a company because where there is growth, there will be openings at many levels. I started as a receiving clerk; a job where I opened boxes and typed invoices. I worked every Saturday in the laboratory, the warehouse, and the receiving department. I learned all I could about the company, their procedures and their products. Then I was promoted to a position in the purchasing department! This was an interesting job. I learned about the importing and exporting side of business. While I was holding the position of Purchasing Assistant, I looked for more ways to advance. *I soon realized that it was the outside sales people who had interesting active jobs, with more freedom in their jobs to pursue other activities/education and to make more money.*

Goal Setting

I decided I was definitely going to move towards a sales career, but I had no experience in sales. So, I began attending many seminars in supervision and business management (both at my own expense and paid for by the company.) Four seminars that Carol Sapin Gold presented were of special interest to me. I showed the Optical Company personnel manager many classes being offered, continually looking for new things to learn. I didn't want to miss any opportunities. Whenever I saw a seminar/course that could help my career I attended it. Even though my career had not yet taken a real positive position, I knew I wanted Sales Management.

It was then that the Avery Class was offered to me. My advice to young women just beginning in business is to take every class, every business seminar they can find, to invest in themselves. We all spend a great deal of money on the outside of our heads. Money spent on improving our minds, learning, growing, is even more valuable.

After one and one-half years, a sales position opened with the Optical Company as a Buyer's Counselor. In the beginning the job consisted of answering complaints, sending correspondence to the consumers, administering government contracts, and handling the mail order side of the business. After two and one-half years, I was advanced to the position of Senior Sales Assistant for the eastern division of the United States. This position was dealing with the manufacturer's representatives.

I had reached a dead end with my Optical Company. There weren't any women as Sales Managers, and after talking with top management I did not feel that they *were open to a woman Sales Manager.* I talked to several other outside companies about obtaining a job as Sales Manager and was told that since I didn't have any direct outside sales experience I was eliminated from *ever* gaining this position.

More Facts

I then went back and asked the top managers if they had been in direct outside sales. They all replied that they had been. *This I feel was a major turning point of my career.* Even though I might have felt safer staying in my current inside position, *I wanted to advance!* I was comfortable where I was, management needed and respected my judgment on many policy matters, and I was satisfied in that I had money, security, and very little pressure. But to reach my new goals I must go out and find a job in outside sales. This decision was very difficult at the time as I didn't have any experience or confidence in myself.

Not wanting to transplant my family, I then decided to look around in the Los Angeles area for a position to use and learn sales skills. This search resulted in my accepting a position at Van De Kamps Bakery in sales management. I was responsible for twenty-two women and thirty-four stores.

I have recently left Van De Kamp's and am employed in sales with a paper company, Blake, Moffitt and Towne. This position is exciting because it is a field that is traditionally all male.

The Wisdom To Know The Difference

As I look back at my career I can see that each place I worked was a learning experience. A bridge to the next opportunity. So I suggest to you that you look at your present job in the same way. How can you learn skills that will make you more valuable, where you are, or to another company? *Never stop moving up! That is how You can be a successful woman! There is lots of room at the top.*

Mary Louise Cutler
965 Grace Street
Northville, MI 48167
(313) 349-8855

MARY LOUISE CUTLER

Mary Louise Cutler has always been active in her community. She is past president of her local club and Assistant District Director of the Business and Professional Women's Club, Inc. She is a Deaconess and lay leader in the Presbyterian church.

Louise was born and reared on a farm in central Iowa. She attended William Penn College where she met her first husband and to that marriage were born four children, twin daughters and two sons. A daughter and son are married and she is a proud new grandmother.

Louise has a vast and varied background of accomplishments. She always accepts a challenge.

She is a graduate of two Dale Carnegie classes and certified for several self-motivational courses.

Her real estate career started in 1966 in Northville, Michigan. She has also served on the Western Wayne Oakland County Board of Realtors for six years and was chosen Realtor-Associate of the Year in 1975. Louise is a member of the Million Dollar Sales Club, one of many ideas she instituted while serving on the Board of Directors of a 4000 member organization.

She married her real estate broker, Jim, in 1970 and they continue to reside in Northville. He has three children and is a grandfather.

Louise left the sales field in 1977, accepting new challenges in the real estate teaching, training and speaking field.

Difficulties often seem to mount and it appears that the horse and wagon part, a symbol of confusion. The superior person meets this situation as a challenge, then sets about bringing order out of disorder. All things progress in a spiraling cycle.

TAO

FROM PAINFUL EXPERIENCES GROW PRECIOUS PEARLS

by Mary Louise Cutler

"The deepest principle in human nature is the craving to be appreciated."

WILLIAM JAMES

"I want a divorce."

The words didn't sound like me, but I was saying them to my husband. Our marriage of sixteen years had fallen apart. Why? First of all I had married a man to please my family. He was a good person but we were not compatible. Our dreams and aspirations were not the same. When my husband would go away on a business trip, I found myself wishing he wouldn't return. How could such a thought ever arise? But it did! I felt so guilty and insecure. Everyone assumed I was a confident person because I attempted to do whatever was asked of me. Inside there was no security and I craved reassurance and approval, especially from my husband and parents.

One evening he informed me that he had been promoted to the main office in Detroit, which would mean no more transfers. My heart sank. I didn't want to leave the Chicago area. My job as a library assistant in a large school district was good and the income was supplemented with a bus route for the special education division. Besides, he had already agreed to a separation.

I rarely expressed my thoughts therefore never discussed the separation with our four children. My husband did, not only with the children but also with my parents. The pressure was put on me. "Mom, everything will be alright when we move," I was told. They were torn and I was torn. Finally, I agreed to move.

I never minded the transfers before. In fact, I looked forward to them. It was a new challenge, a new house to decorate, new people to meet. But the children were tired of it, they never felt settled. I did not look forward to this move.

Arriving in the Detroit area, we contacted various real estate offices and worked with many salespeople even though my heart wasn't in it. They found me exasperating, to say the least! My husband thought if we purchased a more prestigious home it would change my thinking about a divorce. A house could not change my mind! After several trips, we found a house and moved in the middle of November, 1965.

We had lived in Detroit five years previously and knew several families. So, when the new home was in order we invited the personnel from my husband's company to an open house. On the surface everything appeared normal but that sure wasn't the case! I was still going through with the divorce.

To do so required that I learn to be self-sufficient. Without an income producing job I had no security or ability to survive on my own. Two years of college and library assistant experience did not prepare me for a position that could support the children and me. Besides, I was unsure of my own abilities.

The congregation at the small Quaker church where we formerly attended were pleased to have us back, but silently I cried, "Please, please someone notice and help me." During the sermons, tears of frustration rolled down my cheeks. But no one responded. No one could because I wouldn't share my frustrations with anyone, including the minister.

If only someone would have given me what I really wanted and needed—*appreciation!*

> Fear is the most devastating emotion on earth. I fought it and conquered it by helping people who were worse off than I was. I believe that anyone can conquer fear by doing the things he fears to do, provided he keeps doing them until he gets a record of successful experiences behind him.
>
> ELEANOR ROOSEVELT

As had I so many times, my husband believed if you hide from something it will go away. But I learned that life is not that way! One must constantly move forward, set goals and follow new ideas, otherwise you might go deeper and deeper into depression with a resulting nervous breakdown. An inner strength and desire to control my life kept me from such a breakdown. Many hours of prayer and reading inspirational books were my salvation. I lived each day as it came. Nevertheless, there were days of tears and desire for the termination of my life. Thoughts of self destruction through an automobile accident or jumping off a bridge entered my mind, but would I succeed or be left crippled for the rest of my life?

I searched for a purpose of existence. My inner self constantly said, "You've got to keep going. Set a goal, whatever it may be — clean the house, read a good book, help someone less fortunate than yourself." I had set a goal, not the best, but one I would work towards: A divorce — freedom to be myself.

In search of a career I asked a real estate friend about her field. "No problem, just pass the examination, that's all. Come into the office and talk to the broker," was her reply.

"How can a salesperson speak for the broker?" I puzzled.

I waited for the broker's call. One week went by. Nothing. A second week, still no call. I assumed they didn't need me. I fantasized "They don't want me, they won't hire me. I have no experience." Three weeks and still nothing happened. I slipped deeper and deeper into depression. In desperation I convinced myself to take the first step and call them. Dialing that phone number was tough.

My friend answered the phone. Hesitantly I said, "This is Louise. Remember you had mentioned the job as a real estate salesperson — is that position still open?"

"We've been waiting for your call. We thought perhaps you weren't interested."

"I wasn't interested!" I thought to myself. "They had been waiting for my call! Why had I been so hesitant?"

She asked me to wait while she made an appointment with the broker. I was ecstatic! A chance for a job. Did I know how much money it would pay? Absolutely not, but I didn't care anymore. I had to get busy and I felt the real estate field would be a good career as I truly understood people's anticipations and frustrations in moving! An appointment was made for the next day.

What should I wear? I tried several dresses until I found one I felt was right for the interview. I carefully combed my hair, applied my makeup and left in plenty of time for the twenty minute drive. Doubt loomed in my mind and that old insecurity came back. Now wait, I thought, wait and find out what is expected. The butterflies were jumping in my stomach as I entered the office. I was hoping to be reassured by my friend, but she was out on an appointment. The excitement rose and so did the fear, yet I wanted to appear confident. I desperately wanted and needed a job.

The broker quickly put me at ease. "Do you have a car?"

"Yes," I answered.

"Will you be able to work full time?"

"Oh, yes."

"Are you aware that you receive a commission only when someone makes a purchase and the transaction is closed?"

"No, how long does that take?" I cautiously inquired.

"That depends on you. It depends on how much time you're willing to devote to the business."

My mind whirled, "How will I learn all this?"

"We'll train you, but first you must get the state license. Complete this form and send it to the Department of Licensing. They will inform you when to take the examination. Here is a book to study and good luck, Louise!"

I was so excited I could hardly drive home. Now I had something important to do. I read the book, reread it and read it again. I memorized the figures I would need to know. The math problems were difficult to understand so I studied every day for three weeks. I had to pass the test.

The first Monday of February, the designated date, was cold and the roads were slippery. The sun was just coming up as I left for downtown where the examination was held. Finding the building was easy and I went to the large designated room. Five hundred people would be taking the test. The examinations were distributed. My heart raced and my hands were clammy. My body felt warm and my eyes blurred. "If you want to pass this test, you must settle down," I silently told myself. "Relax, take your time." This was easy to say, but it wasn't easy to do. I had *never* enjoyed taking a test! I read each question carefully. If I couldn't understand it, I'd go to the next one and read it carefully. I went through all one hundred questions, one by one. The minutes ticked by. One hour, one and one-half hours, two hours.

Quietly I got up, handed the papers to the monitor and left the room. My waiting had only begun! In a few weeks the license and pocket card would be sent in the mail if we passed. However, if we did not pass we would receive notification in four or five days.

I thought the studying had been hard. Waiting for the mail the next few days was terrible! For the first week each time the mailman came I nervously went to the mailbox and prayed, "Please no card." Death came each time I put my hand into the box. The first day, no card. Second day, no card. Third, fourth and fifth day, no card! Did I dare hope that I had passed? Not doubting me! I worried the sixth, seventh and eighth day!

One day, upon answering the phone, I heard "Congratulations, Louise! Your license and pocket card have arrived. Come in and become acquainted with the office procedures."

I was on cloud nine! A career was starting, a goal had materialized. I had not written it down, but it was foremost in my mind. It taught me that if you really want to do something, go ahead and try. If you put forth the required effort you can obtain it. I was on my way to security and you can find that same feeling. Reach out, catch the "pearl." It's a good feeling!

> Get busy, keep busy. It's the cheapest kind of medicine there is on this earth — and one of the best.
>
> DALE CARNEGIE

The next day in the office the broker informed me of the dues which were required in joining the *Realtor* Board. Also, I would need more clothes as I didn't have the kind that should be worn in an office. Where would I get enough money to cover these costs?

I was visiting a friend and mentioned that I was now in real estate. After congratulating me she also asked for a favor. She and her husband had started a new business building travel trailers and they needed someone to make the curtains. I had sewn for her previously in exchange for my girls' piano lessons, so she knew my ability as a seamstress. I didn't want to sew again, yet, I knew that it would be immediate income. Therefore, I agreed and the business prospered. After about six months I had to hire three additional women to help me. In those early days I would often receive a call for a rush order which meant working in the real estate office all day long, racing home (often after late appointments) and making a set of curtains. Each set required four hours of work. I burned the midnight oil many times.

Soon after I started the sewing job, I met a doctor and asked him about help for my continuing depression. Even though I was working I still had not solved the problem of my insecurity and guilt about wanting a divorce. He recommended taking tranquilizers but I could not accept the false relaxation. I had to keep busy, keep my mind occupied. My therapy was work. I often remember an acquaintance who told me, "Hard work and keeping busy solves many problems." It does!

At about the same time, my doctor mentioned he needed a receptionist for two nights a week from six until eleven. "Good," I thought, "I'll apply for the job. It will give me more additional income." I started a week later.

Three jobs: real estate, the curtain business and doctor's receptionist. The last two gave me cash while I waited for the real estate transactions to close. Real estate was fun and I learned that dressing professionally and making myself look nice helped me feel more secure and important. You, too, will find that regardless of what field you may be employed in, a little makeup and your neat and clean hair can do much to bolster depressed feelings. Remember the days when you were little and dressed up like Mommy or someone you admired? Didn't you feel great? You can still get that same feeling. It just takes a little extra effort. The results will astonish you!

Even though my career(s) was going well, my divorce plans weren't and my husband would still not accept it. This time of life was difficult for all of us in our home. My busy schedule especially affected the children such as the time the girls had tickets to a musical group in Detroit. It was an important evening for them and I had promised to take them, but I received a call from a customer to show a home just before we were to leave. I asked my broker to show the home. The next day when I went into the office the broker said "Your customer made an offer on the house last night and it was accepted."

"Will I receive the commission?"

He answered my thought for me: "Remember, you must show the property to receive commission." I had not shown the property but learned a lesson. I would make appointments for another time, if at all possible. But it was important for my children.

Sadly, too many times I had not considered their feelings first and they fought me. They were just as unhappy and expressed their anger at me. One such incident was when my daughter became engaged after knowing a fellow for only two months. I was furious! She was lashing back at her Mother and I resented it. I tried to explain the benefits of waiting, but she would have none of it. Suddenly I realized that if I didn't fight her she wouldn't feel it necessary to defend herself. So, I started to enthusiastically help her with the wedding plans. As I eased the pressure she was able to be more objective. The wedding did not materialize.

"I can do it, I can do it, if I put my mind to it"

LOUISE CUTLER

By now, my career in real estate was beginning to pay well. In fact I didn't keep track of the money I made from commissions. As it came in I would put into a savings account what I didn't need for clothing, food and utilities. At the end of the year the bookkeeper told me how much I had made in commissions. It was good to be independent.

The summer of 1967 was a highlight of my life. Through the church I was then attending, a tour was available for young people sixteen and over, to visit Europe for twenty-nine days. I asked the twins if they would like to go and offered to pay for half their expenses. They were ecstatic and had the money because they had been babysitters for several years. Unfortunately, the boys were too young to join us. The group required three chaperones of which I was one. When we stayed in hostels or hotels the other female chaperone and myself were bunked with all the girls, including my daughters.

At times the trip was almost unbearable physically and psychologically. I had just filed suit for the divorce before we left and the girls' rejection of me was very evident.

While in Paris, a cold and slight fever kept me in bed while the group went on a sightseeing trip. It was raining and the room was cold and damp. I felt so alone and depressed. "Please, God, end my life," I cried. "I have failed—I don't want to live any longer—I can't go on." The tears continued to stream down my cheeks soaking the pillow.

As the cold receded, I felt better emotionally as well. I tried to keep a positive approach, understand the girls' feelings, let them express themselves and get the bitterness out of their systems.

I remembered when I was young that a friend had told me that whenever I felt low to write her a letter, pour it all out, and by the time she received it I would feel better. I had thought about that many, many times. When you are upset, write it down, put it away and you'll feel better. It works. I know because I finally wrote her that letter while we were in Europe.

Before departing for Europe I resigned my job as receptionist, and upon my return I found that the company for which I had been making the curtains had declared bankruptcy. The two jobs that furnished ready income were gone. I didn't worry though, because by now the real estate was providing a steady income.

The divorce was final November, 1967. The children continued to live with me for two years when the twins graduated from high school and entered college. The two boys then lived with their father and his new wife.

At last I had gained the independence I had desired. I found confidence in my abilities and was proud of my accomplishments as a successful real estate salesperson.

Today, I train people as they prepare for the real estate field. I sometimes look back over the beginning of my real estate career and it frightens me. I wonder, "Would I be able to do the same thing again?" Yes! For I realize that if you really want something, you will do whatever is required! The inner strength will come to you if you're willing to work hard and extend yourself. You *will* be successful. Push yourself and you will overcome each obstacle, one at a time. Like a ladder, go on to the next rung. Each rung takes you to the top. Reach out and grab the "Pearls."

Nancy Reppert
P.O. Box 159
Liberty, MO 64068
(816) 781-7100

NANCY REPPERT

Nancy has spent nearly twenty years in public service due to a conviction that government needs to be concerned about and responsive to citizen needs, while at the same time protecting their rights. She has, thus, advanced into the ranks of top management in the highly male-dominated profession of local government through the fields of law and risk management.

She has 27 years of active service in Boy Scouts of America, ranging from unit positions at every level to Regional Train-the-Trainers experience in a twelve-state region. This experience has included first woman Assistant District Commissioner, first woman Skipper of a Sea Explorer Ship, recruiting and training of adults, counseling of young people and currently the responsibility for creating, developing and implementing a totally new co-ed program concept for high school age young people which, if successful, will become a part of the national program.

Her first book, *Kids Are People, Too,* was published in 1975, and she is working on a second book. Her public speaking career began in the mid-sixties and continues to escalate with a wide diversification of subject. She has had numerous articles published in magazines

She is the recipient of the Award of Merit and Living Sculpture Awards of Boy Scouts of America; member of National Speakers' Association, International Platform Association, United States Naval Institute, Board of Directors of Clay-Platte American Red Cross, National Institute of Municipal Law Officers and Risk and Insurance Managers Society, Kansas City Bar Association Committee on Legal Assistants, National Academy of Arts and Sciences, Fellow of Truman Library Institute and always active in the church, including lay ministry.

She attended Central Missouri State University, UMKC Center for Management Development, Rockhurst College and the University of Arizona; and is currently on the faculty of the Evening Division of William Jewell College. She is married with two grown children and her avocation is skippering sailing yachts and teaching sailing to both adults and young people.

One is strong who conquers others: One who conquers self is mighty.
LAO-TSZE

OYSTER SOUP OR PEARLS— WHICH DO YOU WANT TO CATCH?

by Nancy Reppert

"The Pearl of Potentiality" seems a perfect title for me to consider when writing, since both of the words, "pearl," and "potentiality," have a great deal of meaning for me. My third key word is "stars"; and from those three words hang much of my philosophy of living. There is another word, "diamond," which has its place in the ultimate scheme of my life, and its focus in the pursuit of excellence.

It isn't necessary for me to tell most women that *there is no easy road to success;* but it might be worthwhile to tell them that, even though the road is not easy, *it is there* — and it really doesn't matter how old you are (chronologically), or where you are starting from — *it just matters where you want to go! — And how badly you want to get there!!*

Let's start with the first word — *"pearl."* One of the examples I have used over the years is that of the oyster and the pearl. "No contented oyster ever produced a pearl," I say, "the oyster has to *hurt* before it is able to produce a pearl." This is equally applicable to people. Our lives were never meant to be easy — and the sooner we learn that the most valuable things in our lives are those things which we *know* we have worked hard for and *earned,* the better off we will be. I know of no such thing as a nine-to-five job for one who intends to carve any kind of place for herself. You have to want it badly enough to forget the time, or how much work is involved, or else forget about *being* anybody or anything. No halfway job ever earned anyone any respect.That will only get you a page in "Feebleman's Book of Secondratedness"; and, if you are interested in that philosophy you would not be reading this book. A woman has to do twice as much, and do it twice as well; and in most cases, if you wait for opportunity to be handed to you, you'll still be waiting when you retire. My own experience, and that of most management-level women I know, is that you have to go after every rung on the ladder — but *never* at the expense of others. No one is going to hand you your own business, either; you have to go after it.

I didn't let anyone hold me back, once I got started; but I didn't step on anyone on the way up, either. Obviously, those you step on going up are going to be there waiting for you, if you should start back down. You don't stay up there unless you have the support of those under you; and besides, one of the responsibilities of those who go up is to help others to follow along. I'm not qualified to be a leader unless I'm looking for the best people to follow me, and teaching them how to someday fill my shoes. There have been those who gave me a boost along the way; I have an obligation to do the same for others.

I have learned that I don't want to be contented — at least not for too long at one time. There are plenty of contented folks in the cemetery. It is those who con-

tinuously seek new challenges who are perpetually
young, enthusiastic about life, exciting to be with and who
never really grow old. I don't care how old you are, chronologically; it's never too late to find a new challenge for
your life and go after it. You can be whatever you want to
be, *if* you just want it badly enough to try until you hurt —
and then keep on trying. That's the story of all heroes,
whatever their field. Consider Helen Keller and Wilma
Rudolph, who reached great heights of achievement in
spite of handicaps which would have caused most people to
simply give up and let others take care of them. They
didn't listen to those who said it couldn't be done; they
didn't worry about the odds; they just continued with quiet
determination to try harder, becoming quiet heroes in the
process.

Many women want to get into business or try a career,
but they feel they are too late, too old, or have no experience or skills to sell. In many cases, they have skills they
haven't even considered. One can learn a great deal raising kids and managing a household, if one does it effectively. I learned many of my management skills, and most
of my speaking skills as a volunteer in Scouting — not
Girl Scouts — Boy Scouts of America.

Scouting offered me opportunities to serve — *and* something I could believe in enough to forget about my fears
sufficiently to get up before a group of people and sell them
on volunteering to become Scout leaders. Selling people on
the idea of *paying* to give of their time to others as volun-
teers is not the easiest selling job in the world; but it is said
that I can walk into a room full of people and recruit
everyone there before I walk out again. BSA is a very male
world. It was even more so twenty-seven years ago when I
started; but I learned to function in that world effectively,
and it stood me in extremely good stead in later years
when it became my lot to deal on a professional level with
professional men, and do it as an equal. I cut my professional teeth on the Boy Scout Handbook!

This is a lesson which should never be overlooked.
Women can learn a great deal about all the skills neces-

sary to succeed in the world of business or professions through volunteer service in any one of many fields — and make some very valuable contacts for future entrance into that world.

Scouting also taught me that giving of myself to others was the most satisfying endeavor I could undertake — and the most rewarding. Whatever experience and ability I may have would be of no use whatsoever, if I did not use it for whatever benefit it may provide to others. If I have a light, God did not intend for it to be "hid under a bushel," but set upon a hill — that's what I have tried to do, and what I intend to continue trying to do.

The second word is "*potential.*" Linus, in the comic strip "Peanuts," says, "There is no heavier burden than a great potential." That may be true, but I believe there is no heavier burden than a great potential *unrealized!* There *is* potential in all of us — some of us just don't put forth the necessary effort to realize that potential. For many years I didn't believe I *had* any potential. It took me a long time to realize I did; but once I realized there was some hope for the old girl, I determined to try to find out *how much* — and I haven't found out yet! The point is that God didn't create any of us without a purpose. *There is potential in all of us.* It may be of different sorts and in differing amounts; but it is there, and the difference is how hard we are willing to try. What is the difference between a hero and an ordinary person? Determination! A hero is just an ordinary person *who tries harder!* We all have to learn that before we can even recognize opportunity, because opportunity is nearly always disguised as hard work, risk and sacrifice. That oyster never had any potential other than oyster soup until it hurt — *that* was when it started producing the pearl!

The pearl, itself, however, is only *potential* until it is discovered and extracted from the oyster. It has no real value until the oyster gives it up. *Most of the potential in people must be "given away" before it has any real value.* The Bible tells us a talent which is buried will never grow or multiply and is of little real use or value to anyone.

Many of us bury our potential — or let others bury it for us — and, therefore, never allow it to realize its value. That is a crime against God and all of those people who might benefit from our pearls of potentiality, *if* we just dig them up and start giving them away.

I didn't bury mine, so much as I allowed others to bury them by believing those who told me I had none. I know what it is to bring myself up from the depths, so I know others can, too. And saying it's too late, or you're too old, is just a "cop-out." I didn't even start picking myself up until I was past thirty-five, didn't get even a faint hope of success til I was past forty, and didn't become really self-actualizing until I was past forty-five. Many have started and succeeded much later in life than I.

There were many people who contributed to the "opening of the oyster" because they believed there just might be a pearl inside. Among them are my two children, Jay and Tracy, who not only believed in me, but made it necessary for me to keep trying; my husband, John, who has been ever supportive; Dr. Wilbur T. Hill, who was probably the first to try to "pry open the oyster" because he believes there is potential in everyone; Jim Wirken and Rick Morrison, attorneys and instructors in my law courses, who demanded excellence in terms of both effort and product; Conn Withers, who first urged me to try the law, also demands excellence, and constantly supported my efforts as I worked under his direction; and, finally, Charles Swanson Anderson, who would never be satisfied with just a pearl, if he thought enough heat and pressure just might produce a diamond in its place. All of these people, and more, were my "stars"; and that is where the third word comes in.

Even before I became a sailor, I had taken as a personal tenet for my life a quote I once read — "If you would walk among the stars,then you must walk with those who walk among the stars." Street signs and road maps are necessary to the land-bound traveler so that he may find his way in, or to strange places. Sailors have, for centuries, used the stars as their "street signs and road maps" across the trackless seas to ports they may only have dreamed of; but they know what their goal is, and how to use the stars to find their way.

I wanted to challenge the ultimate limits of my potential; that was my goal — but I needed some guide — some "road map" to find my way. I chose people who exemplified the qualities I wanted to acquire and I tried to learn what made them outstanding in my judgment. Then I set out to become what I wanted to be through study, determination, observation, and risk-taking, forcing myself to do just the things I feared most to do (which is, of course, the true definition of courage and the only road to success).

I chose my "stars" to guide me, and I set out to reach new and more challenging ports of call. I found that all of my "stars" had many things in common. They were people who always put forth *extraordinary positive effort* in whatever they did. They were people who were not satisfied to be exceptional in just their chosen professions, but also involved themselves deeply in civic and volunteer activities, while still finding time for their families and their churches. They filled their lives with positive endeavor and gave of themselves freely. They fitted my definition of heroes — they were mostly ordinary people who tried harder. I found that *they had all refused to settle for anything less than quality and excellence in what they did,* and expected nothing less from those who worked with or for them. They set an example and they expected it to be followed. They had value to impart; they knew it, and they wanted to share it. People are meant to give of themselves — and the only truly happy people I have known are those who do. The only reason I write and speak is because I believe I have something of value to say to others; something of value to give. That was the purpose of my book, *Kids Are People, Too;* and it has been the reason for every talk I have ever made and all of the satisfying work I have ever done.

Women must know they are only "down" when they let themselves be down — that they *can do* anything, if they are only willing to seek out opportunities— in the form of hard work, risk, courage, sacrifice, determination, striving, and maybe most of all doing what one really believes in. Opportunity doesn't come knocking at your door begging you to come out. You have to find it, chase it, tackle it, and wrestle it to the ground — *then* convince it *you* are the one it was really looking for. Professional and managerial risk-taking is usually one of the hardest things for women to learn; but it is a pre-requisite for an effective manager and decision-maker.

I return to the stars! Most of my courage, and management and decision-making skills have resulted from two things — sailing and six years of endurance trails working with Charles S. Anderson, the man who never heard of second best — and would never settle for even a pearl, if there was any possibility that something better might be forced to the surface with enough effort and pressure. If you were going to stay on the same team with this man, you'd better be ready to go "hell bent for leather" in the pursuit of excellence, because he would settle for nothing less. He didn't offer a whole lot; but he demanded a lot. He appealed to our pride, not to our natural inclination to seek security. He simply set a quiet example of dedication and excellence which we could do no less than attempt to emulate. He could never brook mediocrity, nor would he be tolerant of anything less than the best that was within us. People grow only when challenged and he was remorseless in his demands; but, because of that, the slightest hint of approval from him was more valuable to us than lavish praise from a lesser light, because we knew what he expected in the way of excellence — and that he did not give even the smallest praise lightly. He refused to allow us to take things personally and he forced us to debate issues with all the determination we had. He wanted us to argue with him, if we believed in our position; if he was wrong, he wanted to know. He didn't want any "yes men" or "yes women" in his organization. He took ordinary people and *turned them into extraordinary people,* because he expected nothing less, and each of us was determined not to be the one to let him down. Such a person brings out only the best in the people who work with him, and so he did.

I know about the stars. I still look for them; but they have to be bigger and brighter now, because I've sailed far from the port where I embarked. I am younger now than I was at twenty-five; I have more energy, drive, determination, courage, confidence, and skills; more of everything which makes life worth living and less of the things which make it hard to bear. I have learned that, as Morris West wrote in "Shoes of the Fisherman," "It takes so much to be a full human being that there are very few who have the enlightenment or the courage to pay the price . . . One has to abandon altogether the search for security and reach out to the risk of living with both arms. One has to embrace the world like a lover. One has to accept pain as a condition of existence. One has to court doubt and darkness as the cost of knowing. One needs a will stubborn in conflict, but apt always to total acceptance of every consequence of living and dying."

I have recently been charged with the responsibility of creating and developing a completely new program concept for high school age young people for Boy Scouts of America, and implementing the pilot program. I'm hiking, backpacking, rappelling down cliffs and climbing back up them, and canoeing down rivers. Not just keeping up with teenaged kids, but leading them, earning their respect and building a program which I sincerely hope will someday serve kids all over the United States by helping them to find personal development, team-building and trust-level development, and leadership development for themselves and for the future of this country.

Kids are the future; but there are millions of women out there who think, as I once thought, that their lives are over, when they haven't really begun yet. The "Pearl of Potentiality" is nothing if it is never anything but potential. All things are difficult before they are easy, but there is potential in all of us. It will never become a pearl, or a diamond, without sufficient pressure, some suffering, some hurt, a lot of striving, a lot of caring, a lot of giving and a willingness to take risks — a lot of them — in short, a willingness to *try harder!* A single reason why you *can* do something is worth a hundred reaons why you can't.

"Let us not ever," as Voltaire said, "be guilty of the things we did not do"; and *we never know what we can do unless and until we try.* It is no sin to fail; it is useless never to try. Ideals are like stars; you will not succeed in touching them with your hand, but like the seafarers, you choose them as your guides, and following them you reach your destiny. Idealists, foolish enough to throw caution to the winds, have advanced humankind and enriched the world, and little real progress has ever been made without controversy and criticism. Women will cause and endure their share, but history shows that those individuals who are strongly committed to excellence, truth, honor, and honesty ultimately prevail.

We are all God's pearls of potentiality — He didn't create us without purpose; but I don't believe He meant it to be easy, either. None of the things which are best and most valuable is ever achieved easily or without hurt; but we were meant to be of value on this earth, or God would not have put us here. Albert Schweitzer said, "God has no sons who are not servants"   that's truc of His daughters, too.

Julee Goodman
4530 N. 110th Street
Milwaukee, WI 53225
(414) 464-7033

JULEE GOODMAN

Julee has charisma. She can relate to others because she has personally encountered both sides. Her entrance into the field of human development came after her own experience in overcoming severe mental depression in the early adult years of her life.

During the past 20 years, Julee has developed her skills as a trainer, counselor and motivational speaker. She designs and conducts attitude awareness seminars and courses for corporations, educational and governmental agencies and convention audiences. Her greatest talent lies in her ability to help men, women and young people from all walks of life increase their self-esteem and understanding of others—Major corporations and individuals alike report dramatic results in increased personal and professional happiness and productivity.

Currently she is an active member of the American Society for Training and Development, President of Total Living Concepts, and a certified coordinator for Personal Dynamics Institute of Minneapolis. She is also a member of both the Wisconsin and National Speakers Associations.

Julee inspires many as a volunteer motivational speaker for United Way fund raising campaigns of Greater Milwaukee. She is a frequently sought after guest on television and radio talk shows.

Several of Julee's seminars—"The Ultimate Woman" and "Light Up Your Life" are designed especially for women's audiences. Her expertise in this area of personal development was further heightened in recent years through her affiliation with the John Robert Powers Modeling and Finishing Agency, focusing on *total living concepts* for women.

A time of adversity can lead to success. When one becomes calm and remains cheerful all through the time of danger, it creates a cornerstone of confidence for all those about one to build upon. Thus one's example becomes the very fountainhead of subsequent success.

TAO

HOW I TURNED STRESS INTO SUCCESS

by Julee Goodman

As a wounded oyster mends its shell by creating a pearl, little could I know my overwhelming handicap was to become my greatest strength . . . That those two dreaded words *mental illness* were to be the grains of sand that would eventually bring forth the "Pearl of Potentiality" in my life.

This is written with the sincere hope of helping the millions of men, women and children who are bewildered by the devastating affects of nervous or mental illness and the discouragement it causes in their own lives and in the lives of everyone close to them.

My regained mental health is the *success* I value above all other!

It took hard work, courage to fail many times and begin again, and unconditional acceptance of myself and others.

"Strength is not born of strength, but of weakness." No matter what your past or present condition is or *how long* you have been suffering—*you can get well!*

You cannot help the way you *feel*, but you *can control* the way you *think* and *act!*

Control of your thoughts and actions through *patient practice* will, without fail, eventually bring renewed self-respect and health!

What is now your greatest weakness can become *your* gleaming "Pearl of Potentiality"!

A Formidable Phantom

. . . It was early summer shortly before my 21st birthday. Strange, unexplainable changes began to take place inside and around me. It seemed as though my reliable and heretofore unnoticed inner workings had gone *out of control!* Flashing panics would come and go—familiar people and places felt unreal to me, as though I was on the outside looking in. Something terrifying was happening, but whatever it was seemed unexplainable, unlike anything I had ever experienced before!

I hadn't done anything unusual, yet I couldn't shake off this morbid, gnawing inner sense of *worthlessness and guilt!*

I became afraid to look at sharp objects—formerly harmless household items began to shriek of *danger*—scissors, kitchen knives, Lysol, Iodine—everyday cleaning products labeled "poison" tormented my mind. Where were these screaming impulses to *end my life* coming from? I often foolishly even tried to hide the threatening bottles and objects from myself. I longed for the *peace* death would bring . . . *how long could I go on like this* . . . Suicide hurts the people left behind! . . . I don't want to hurt anybody — *God! I don't want to hurt anybody!* . . . but I'm scared to death I might if this doesn't go away!

What was wrong? . . . Was anything wrong?—It was all so vague and unclear—where could I go for help for a thing like this? Maybe I don't need any help—sometimes it seems to let up . . . *I'll be all right* . . . this will pass over as things always do . . . and on and on and on . . . My tormented mind *ached for understanding!*

In the beginning when these strange feelings first started, my husband and I thought something had possibly gone wrong physically. Prior to the onset of the above, I had had painful burning sensations in my chest and stomach—ulcers, perhaps? . . . The doctor suggested we not waste the money on x-rays. "It's just your nerves," he said. "Just take this medication and buy yourselves a new living room chair." (He knew we had only been married for a short time!) The medication made me feel tired, but not better. Again and again to doctors. Again and again — "Just nerves"!

If it hadn't happened to me personally, I could never have understood this strange mysterious phantom as I do now.

I had a good job in display advertising on a daily newspaper and my creative and ambitious young husband, Bob, and I had been married only a little over a year. Although we both had said and meant, "Until death do us part," I knew neither of us had bargained for anything like this!

Why? As a supposedly normal, healthy, 21 year old woman, could I no longer even get out of bed in the morning, walk to my mailbox or fill an empty sugar bowl . . . without feelings of terrifying fear, exhaustion and despair?

Routine tasks became almost impossible. Getting ready for work took all the energy I could muster. All interest in my previously well-groomed appearance was gone! I repeatedly found myself wearing the same dreary grey wool suit or green flowered dress day after day.

My job became confusing and difficult. Laying out or writing copy for even a small, simple advertisement for a local merchant seemed too much for me! Trembling and nausea became my constant companions—I'd try to look like I was just fine, but inside my feelings of fear and

depression screamed *there was something wrong!*
Some undefinable danger! I tried desperately not to let
others see what was going on inside me. In shame *I carefully hid my inner feelings from even our closest friends
and relatives.*

One afternoon I became so frightened and desperate, I
cried hysterically, in spite of trying with everything in me
to hold back the tears. A co-worker in the office took me
home and called my husband.

I took a leave of absence from my job with a mixed sense
of shame and relief, but in the hope that I would soon be
back to work again.

My mind would race wildly until a feeling of pressure
would build in my head to what seemed like a breaking
point, but at the same time my mind seemed dead, as if
incapable of thinking at all. As weeks and months went
by, feelings swung wildly from hope to despair.

Sleep became my only escape. But even that was changing. Night after night I would go to bed hopefully to rest
my weary mind and body. Usually I was so tired I would
fall asleep immediately, only to awaken three or four
hours later with panic flashing through my body. Falling
back to sleep as I had been accustomed to doing earlier
became less and less frequent. How was I going to handle
this? Some nights my heart would pound, but I would try
to lie quietly so not to awaken Bob. I feared that the worry
my bizarre feelings would cause might make him and
others in our family nervous and ill too. Mostly, deep
inside, I feared he would no longer be able to love me and
tolerate this strange intruder in our marriage.

We prayed for a baby—we felt sure that this wonderful
new addition to our lives would bring about just what was
needed to get my mind off myself and my inner turmoil.

My Prayers Felt Flat and Stale

All the things I used to do with ease, preparing dinner,
ironing a shirt, visiting a neighbor, answering a phone,

even holding a baby! ... Everything seems so unreal and frightening!
I'm *afraid to die* ... but I'm even more *afraid to live* ...
Oh, please God! Take this away and help me be like I used to be!
What was happening? Was I losing my mind? I had never *tried* harder and it seemed the harder I tried the stronger my nameless phantom became. This phantom of fear that seemed as real as if it were constructed of concrete and steel.

By this time my husband and the few others I had tried to share my feelings with were also discouraged and bewildered with my inability to *once and for all* rid myself of this inconvenient and mysterious visitor that had invaded our lives.

Patience and understanding had grown short. The doctors had found the answer: Emotional Blocks, deep seated Anxiety Neuroses and Severe Depression. These terms alone frightened me, but the thing that turned *fear* into *terror* was the fact that my family, myself, *not even my doctors* seemed to know what to do to avoid these strange recurrences ... "Unstable Childhood," "Poor Mental Health Environment," "Sensitive Nervous System." These were the explanations.

It's No Wonder

... My childhood and adolescent years had the usual ups and downs, perhaps a few extras as my parents were divorced when my brother, Ron, and I were at an early age. The following were somewhat uncertain years for us. Living for various periods of time with our grandparents, Mother and Dad, stepparents and other close relatives and friends. By graduation from high school I had attended over a dozen different schools.

In retrospect I would admit there were some painful and difficult times. Always having to leave behind friends and relationships that had only begun.

I occasionally felt a deep sense of not really belonging. Not being quite like the others. Although I was averagely popular, I felt alone and different at times. I took no special notice of these feelings, although I was aware of their presence . . . That was all in the past . . . What was to become of the future?

At times my feelings would lift! There were days, sometimes weeks at a time when I felt like my old self . . . *I knew I was well!* Life could go on again, I would make plans and decisions for our future! Invite friends over for dinner, clean closets, write letters, all the things I had so sorely neglected.

A Case of Misunderstanding

Wrong! The feelings would descend again, sometimes stronger than ever. Panic, depression, inability to concentrate—sometimes I couldn't remember the simplest things, the name of a life long friend, a remark that had just been made or the content of a single sentence I had just read. I was constantly rummaging through self-help books and articles hoping to find the answer!

I feared my personality and memory were disintegrating. Little could I realize then that my faulty memory would come back to become *better than ever!* That in years to come I would be writing and conducting seminars for large numbers of participants and would develop a remarkable ability to remember names and handle day-long lectures and group discussions with ease, as I do now.

Little did I understand at that time that my strange and unacceptable feelings, thoughts, impulses and sensations were *not* indications *of a weak character,* only *a vulnerable nervous system responding to life's tensions with painful symptoms.*

Later I came to know there had been no *organic* damage to my aching mind. That only its *function* had been disturbed by my fear and preoccupations with ideas of shame and danger. I had become so absorbed with my inner torment that I was no longer concentrating on what was going on around me. Insult was being added to injury through my belief that my character must be weak for such *a humiliating condition to have taken over my life!* Later I was to learn that it would take *far more* than average character and *will* to bear the discomfort to practice with patience *self-acceptance and determination* to regain my balance on the "tight-rope" of life.

We would scarcely blame an athlete for his inability to run on a broken leg, or an ulcer victim for his sensitive digestive system. Both the sufferer, family and friends could easily comprehend the problem at hand and offer helpful assistance and patient acceptance. When a person becomes physically ill, cards, flowers, candy and loving concern are a natural response.

Such is often not the case with mental and emotional suffering—once a condition has been diagnosed as "just nerves" we naturally assume it is "all in the mind." The patient is often admonished to practice taking a more positive outlook on life. "Fight" whatever it is that's bothering him, or just plain "snap out of it"! He has attempted repeatedly to "fight" and to correct his faulty thinking only to find he is no longer any match for the disturbing unwanted feelings that seem to speak a frightening and demoralizing language all their own! There are no visible casts or bandages to hold emotional suffering in place while it heals—only insight, patience, understanding and love!

Despite the giant strides medical science continues to make, emotional illness is still among the least understood and most misunderstood of all human afflictions.

Why is there such a lack of acceptance and understanding in spite of dramatic breakthroughs in other areas of human suffering?

I remember at the age of 15 remarking after the suicide of a nervously ill friend, "I could be many things, but I'm sure I could never *let* myself get that depressed!" At that time I thought depression was a *choice*—not an illness.

After experiencing and overcoming many years of severe depression and chronic anxiety in my own life and after over 20 years of counseling and working with others seeking help, as well as presenting seminars involving thousands of homemakers, business and professional people from every walk of life — I offer this concrete possibility.

Could the difficulty in understanding be because we cannot *see* or *feel* what goes on *within* another individual? Most illnesses have a tangible "cause" or "reason," some clearly defined beginning and end—Mental and Nervous conditions linger on, disappear and reappear when least expected to again harass the weary victim and his family.

I Won and So Can You!

It became evident that what I was in need of was not more character or a new nervous system, but merely the tools to help me strengthen the sensitive, but thoroughly reliable and respectable ones I had been born with. For many years the *stigma* of my inner feelings and impulses had prevented me from any longer respecting myself.

If only I had known at that time that I was not responsible for the *feelings* that came to my mind (No matter how ugly or undesirable). But—that I *could* and would learn to *control my thoughts* and *actions* and through this simple, though not easy, practice regain inner peace and balance in my life. I could command my "muscles" to *act!* . . . to get out of bed, dress myself neatly and do at least a few of the tasks that needed to be done—and give myself credit for the extreme effort involved!

For short periods of time, bursts of insight would try to break through my mental confusion. In these all too brief intervals I would again become aware of a potentially worthwhile person inside me. I remembered reading the promise that the "Kingdom of God was within every person" — Maybe even *me!* . . . Could it be God has no stepchildren, no grandchildren and no children too *ill or confused* to be loved?

But that was part of the big question in my mind that kept coming back with pushy aggressive self-doubt. Was I possibly *ill?*—or was this just something I was doing to myself? I felt as though I had become *allergic* to life and people, particularly to *myself!*

. . . I was to later learn that what I *was* allergic to was *tension!* . . . and that I would find ways to reduce its harmful affects on my nervous system.

. . . *Would I ever be like I used to be* . . . *FREE of this Phantom of Torment?*

My answer came! I finally realized I had been asking God to do *for* me what I had to do for myself! That God could only do *for* me what He could do *through* me!

My prayers changed! . . .

"Please, God, show me HOW to overcome this formidable phantom and if there are others who are confused and hurting inside like I am, use me if you can to help them find their way too!"

But *how?* Psychiatrists had already indicated that the causes of my present problem had their roots somewhere deep in early childhood . . . and that I would simply have to learn to live with it!

It was clear the *past* could not be altered, but what about the *future?* For *over eight years now* I had been trying in every way I knew to overcome my fears and depression!

It Would Take a Miracle!

Webster's dictionary defines a miracle as, "A wonderful happening." At this point one started to take place in my life!

It was January of 1959. The evening paper in our city carried an article that caught my attention. *"Emotionally ill patients help cure one another."* It was announcing a systematic, self-help method called *Recovery, Inc.* As I read on, the article told how it had been founded and developed by a Chicago psychiatrist and neurologist in 1937. Dr. Abraham Low, it stated, had for many years served as Assistant Director of the Psychiatric Institute of the University of Illinois Medical School in Chicago.

The doctor's purpose in establishing these self-help training groups, it explained, was not to supplant the physician, but to provide a systematic method by which suffering patients could *get well and stay well.* Dr. Low, the article stated, often lovingly referred to his patients as "My dear ones"!

My hopes soared! It all made sense! I had been through the merry-go-round of psychiatrists and doctors of every description with only short-lived, if any, relief. One psychiatrist had told me that the more sensitive and responsive one happened to be, the more likely they were to be affected by my type of suffering. I wasn't sure why at the time, but that doctor's comment helped me more than any I'd heard. Later I understood *why.* It had soothed my painful fear of stigma and character indictment and gave me *hope and dignity.*

As I read further, the newspaper reporter's quotes from Dr. Low's textbook for patients, "Mental Health Through Will Training," sounded as if the doctor was speaking directly to me!

He trained his patients to understand they are suffering from *Nervous Symptoms.* Very distressing, often to the point of excruciating torture, he pointed out, but *never dangerous.* There are *no hopeless cases,* difficult, yes, but none are hopeless *no matter how long they have been ill.*

The article stated that patients are helped to *get well* and quiet their painful fear of stigma when they learn to understand that they are suffering from a very average human illness . . . and it is *no disgrace to become ill.*

No disgrace to be *ill?* Perhaps I really had been ill and not just weak and wrong for feeling as I had all those years, and *no hopeless cases!* Maybe, not even me!

A Living Legacy

Then my heart sank as my eyes fell on the following words. Dr. Low had died in 1954. It was now 1959, over five years after his death. *I was too late!* But, *no!* This remarkable doctor had left a *living legacy* to his patients for years to come, *Recovery, Incorporated.* He had carefully developed and supervised these self-help groups throughout the country for over 17 years before his death, and there were several meetings each week in our community.

Again my hopes soared! My husband and our three beautiful children: Greg, three, Beth, two, and Mike, our new four-month old baby son needed a wife and mother to *walk* not *crawl* through life with them.

In late January of 1959 I became a member of Recovery, Inc. I attended every meeting without fail and as I began to regain my own health, was appointed and trained to become leader of the group I was attending in Kalamazoo, Michigan. My hungry, aching mind devoured every principle I could put into practice in my life.

I was surprised to see *people from every walk of life* at these meetings . . . homemakers, business and professional men and women, even members of the clergy and religious orders. It was interesting to find religion seems to neither increase or decrease the likelihood of emotional illness.

Most important of all, I was trained to recognize and change my *habit patterns* of thinking—to become *aware* of the many shades of *anger* and *fear* that produced the *tension that was keeping my nervous suffering alive!* Without the fuel of sustained *tension,* I found nervous symptoms would rise, fall , and soon die away. The illness had created difficult habit patterns—progress was slow, setbacks were many—but all were beginning to change with *insight, patient practice* and *acceptance!*

Acceptance

In spite of even severe recurrances of symptoms, I was learning *how* I could *change my thoughts,* replace insecurity with security. How to recognize when I was thinking or acting in *negative extremes* and bring my *attitudes* back into healthy *positive* balance.

The discovery that I had *so much anger* was surprising and unappealing to me (even though anger is a basic and necessary human emotion). I had always been a *super-pleaser* type person, concerned abut being liked and cared a great deal what others thought about me.

I didn't know I was *mad at anybody,* but I was! Most of all at *myself* for being ill and at others for not seeming to care or understand how much I was hurting inside and how desperately hard I had been trying to get well. Such a strange dichotomy. I wanted their love and understanding but I was too afraid and vulnerable to communicate my need because I feared if they really knew me, and how I felt inside, they might not like the type person they would see. So I tried to hide the real me with all my real, though sometimes confused, feelings and thoughts.

Finally, my insight came to a point where my mind could *forgive* and *accept* everybody once and for all. Dr. Low called it to *"excuse not accuse."* My parents, my husband, my family and friends, and the constant flow of every-day irritations and frustrations that living brings. I was becoming more patient and less judgmental with people and things around me . . . including *myself!* I began to try to give my family and friends what I needed most: *respect, encouragement and appreciation.* Whether they gave it back to me or not.

The whole key to "excusing not accusing" for me was the full realization that most people don't even understand themselves, so how could I expect them to understand me? That if they hurt me or seem uncaring it is because they themselves are hurting or in need of understanding. An over-simplification, perhaps, but that's the way I now see it, and that point of view, more than any other, has lifted tenseness from my previously overly burdened nervous system and has changed my life from dismal years of *chronic anxiety and depression* to what has since become over *15 years of radiant health and success.*

As Christ said so simply, . . . "Forgive them, Father, for they know not what they do."

How could I any longer expect others to understand what I had gone through inside when it was so thoroughly "un-understandable"—even to me!

How difficult it is to be a relative or friend. Relatives and friends are only human too. *We need to help each other understand,* not fight against one another in frustration, anger, fear and self-defense.

I accepted and understood finally that *I had not been responsible for becoming ill,* but that *I and I alone could and did take full responsibility for learning how to get myself well!* The promise had come true . . . "Seek and ye shall find." . . . and I did . . .

In recent years many new self-help organizations have emerged throughout the world—although quality of leadership and method should be carefully considered, I strongly endorse their potential value for the following reasons: 1. Low cost enables often necessary long-term training and reinforcement for the sufferer. 2. For some reason, the group system is able to accomplish what is often impossible in a one-to-one, doctor-patient relationship. I am certain I would not have reached the final cure had I continued only to see private psychiatrists. Cost was high and results were short lived.

My turning point came in learning *how* to get well, not *why* I had been ill. I would like to point out here that my story relates just *one type* of emotional illness. There are, of course, many, many others. I have seen self-help group training enable many so-called "hopeless cases," such as I, to regain and maintain mental and emotional heath.

I am not an unusual or particularly gifted person in any way. *What worked for me can work for you.* In all honesty, I attribute my present insight and inner peace to the self-help training and the continued effort to keep studying and searching to find my way. For seventeen years, until 1975, I led self-help training, seeing myself and countless others again find health and happiness.

A New Life

Some of my greatest fears at that time have become my outstanding joys and strengths as I *practiced doing the things I had feared to do.* I found the more I attempted, regardless of fear of failure, *the more I became capable of accomplishing.*

For over 21 years I have experienced the final part of that prayer of long ago. The opportunity to "help others as I helped myself," to build healthy, happy, productive lives. My own background, constant study and working with others has proven to me how alike all we different people are!—Our inner needs and problems vary only in degree and intensity!

I am president of my own company, Total Living Concepts, and over the past four years have developed, marketed and presented Attitude Awareness Seminars and Human Growth Programs for corporations and individuals . . . helping people to *get excited about themselves and their capacity to help others around them become aware of their full capabilities!*

"The Ultimate Woman" and "Light Up Your Life" are two programs I have designed especially for women's audiences. Both combine interesting and fascinating techniques to help each woman achieve her ultimate potential and realize a greater degree of personal and professional satisfaction and fulfillment in her life. These seminars are presented in the Milwaukee area and throughout the country.

How to Start Your New Beginning . . .

Dr. Abraham A. Low was a pioneer in the development of self-help. Today there are many other self-help community resources available throughout the world.

Your local Mental Health Association can give you this information, or write:

Recovery, Inc.
116 South Michigan Avenue
Chicago, Illinois 60603

(Over 1000 Recovery groups are currently available throughout the United States, Canada, Puerto Rico and Ireland.)

Today, every bookstore is overflowing with "Self-Help" publications . . . Below are several suggested readings I have found to be among the best:

Claire Weekes, M.D., *Peace from Nervous Suffering,* and *Hope & Help for Your Nerves* (Hawthorne).

Abraham A. Low, M.D., *Mental Health Through Will Training* (Christopher Publishing House)

John A. Schindler, M.D., *How To Live 365 Days a Year* (Fawcett Crest)

. . . I sincerely wish I could meet *every one* of you . . . to give you *help* when you feel hopeless and *hope* when you feel helpless . . . remember, *I won and so can you!*

LaRee Foster
P.O. Box 56
Radcliffe, IA 50230
(515) 899-2100

LaRee FOSTER

LaRee Foster grew up in Jefferson, Iowa, where she met her husband, Paul. They are parents of three grown children. One son farms and a son and daughter are enrolled at Oral Roberts University.

After many years in direct selling and helping other women achieve their goals, LaRee has founded *Genesis Point*. As President, LaRee guides her associates in workshops tailored to the needs of the organization. Referral consultants in Genesis Point serve varied needs of clients. Her own seminars challenge women to capture a vision of their potential. She is still very actively involved in designing and coordinating sales training sessions. During her limited spare time LaRee has written many "Sunshine" booklets on direct selling and motivation. Other publications include original calendars for clients, a cookbook and her poetry. She is currently organizing the first chapter of the National Organization of Women Business Owners in the state of Iowa.

Believing that if you can see the invisible you can do the impossible, LaRee urges all women to capture a vision of what can be.

17

By the accident of fortune a person may rule the world for a time, but by virtue of love one may rule the world forever.
LAO-TSZE

I CAN!

by LaRee Foster

I must have been born screaming "I can!" One of my earliest recollections was proclaiming to my family, "I can so be a mountain-climber if I want to!" Logic and ridicule could not dissuade my childish proclamations. I knew I could! That attitude has been put to the test many times. I've climbed many "mountains" and fallen from countless "cliffs." My life, perhaps like yours, has been neither totally triumphant nor relentlessly tragic.

Therein lies my message to you. It is in my sameness that I am one with you. All our lives, physical and mental growth patterns have been preparing and strengthening us for the most beautiful time of life—now.

From the beginning, my genesis, the warp and the woof of my life, has been the intricate weaving of various people and numerous details. Singular and seemingly isolated events have all been part of the master plan. Oblivious to this plan and despite my rebellion, *God made the stumbling blocks into stepping stones.* The times of my life have indeed been in His hands. Believing that, I can rest assured that the burden and bliss of growth will continue. For each moment becomes a magical opportunity to expand my possibilities if I but reach out towards my dream. A new day is a fresh link of time related to the past, but receptive to the purposeful plan for the future.

Words to a popular song say, "If you don't have a dream, how ya' gonna make a dream come true?" The writer knew that nothing happens until the flicker of a dream is born in our hearts. A dream kept before us will give character to our days and creativity to our meditations.

James Allen, author of *As a Man Thinketh,* exhorts us to: "Dream lofty dreams and your dreams you shall become." We become what we dream, so pick your dream carefully.

At an early age I became very aware of the importance of claiming and maintaining a dream. Before me every day I saw my father keep on dreaming, although circumstances did not always encourage dreams. His daily example of stretching his energy, financial resources, and imagination to encompass a new dream has been an invaluable lesson to me all my life. Holidays always brought us real-life stories of his depression childhood. It was then I learned that looking beyond present circumstances and capturing a vision of the future provides the energy to complete the task before us.

During my pre-teen years I found that dreams helped me "get going," but dreams demand schemes and a commitment to pursue a goal without giving up. To keep on keeping on is the task set before us to prove our dream.

My early goals were simple: make enough money so I would not have to ask for a nickel every time I became thirsty for Dad's Old-fashioned Root Beer. I did not realize the need for the money as much as I knew I would enjoy the freedom from asking for it. I was willing to work for that independence.

Since, at age ten, there were few white collar jobs available, I pounded the pavement, door-to-door, with a brown grocery sack filled with boxes of greeting cards. After school and hot summer days, I knocked on doors. For three years I was patronized, yelled at, ignored; but more importantly I was earning money! I discovered that a working commitment, knocking on every door on every street, was what put the dollars in my pocket. Success felt great, but I soon found out "feeling" did not make money, only working did.

I bought a bicycle and pedaled my greeting cards into my teen years. It was during this time I discovered one step better than the pride of persistence in your work was to have someone notice! This revelation came my way when I volunteered to be a "go-fer" for a big community project, knowing the only way a gangly "nobody" would be noticed was to position myself close to the Chairlady and work harder and smarter than everyone else.

And work I did! Not a penny was paid me, but I became wealthy through that experience. I had earned the title of "Girl Friday." A job well-done and recognition for it; what heady food to inspire the soul.

The recognition I received taught me that we make our own opportunities using the tools of desire, hard work, and determination.

Appreciation of my efforts as "Girl Friday" took a substantial form by the next summer. A national company contacted the local Chamber of Commerce asking the Chamber to recommend a friendly, hard-working girl to demonstrate their products throughout central Iowa. The day they hired me was a triumph of persistence. I was not the prettiest or the smartest, but I was prepared when opportunity presented itself.

Always believing that I could achieve something extraordinary if I could dream it, and putting that together with committed effort, made possible my first "public" position. It was hard and sometimes scary work, but like selling door-to-door, I had the opportunity to meet all kinds of people. Every new personality presented a challenge; a sale became a victory; each new day afforded me an open-ended opportunity to do my part, be my best and give my utmost. It was I who benefited and grew toward my vision of tomorrow! Approaching the end of my teen years I was sure that I would always fly straight as an arrow to the target. My goals were all set and I was ready to take on anything. Remember those mountains I planned to climb? The reality of those mountains became a desire to teach and share with others my belief that we can live graciously with others and comfortably with ourselves while enthusiastically pursuing our goals.

Never doubt for a moment your ability to ultimately achieve your goals. The road to success is often via detours, but those sideroads are filled with unlimited opportunities.

It was in retrospect that I discovered the problem of the moment was the key to the solution for my future goal. I did not recognize at the time that "giving up" my dreams to marry a handsome young man and have children disguised the greatest opportunity of all.

"And the greatest of these is love . . ."

During these years, formative for both our children and me, I began to understand how *it is only in giving that we receive* and in loving that we grow to our full stature. If we have true love which "beareth all things, believeth all things, hopeth all things, endureth all things," (1 Corinthians 13:7), we are preparing ourselves for the opportunity to help others; thereby reaching toward our fulfilled potential.

Love must be a vital force in our lives; else we are not open to the joys and sorrows, the excitements and the quiet strength love offers us. Without this ingredient on the abundant platter of life we could die long before our burying. The only truly pitiable people I have ever known are those who do not understand:

> Love ever gives
> Forgives—outlives
> And ever stands
> With open hands.
> And while it lives,
> It gives.
> For this is love's prerogative,
> To give and give and give.

The opportunity to learn to love my husband, Paul, and our three marvelous children, Jay, Paul III, and Lori, has been a priceless gift. And where better to practice this gift than in that very intimate relationship . . . caring for my family. Yet, the very nature of my wife-mother job left time, though it had to be cultivated, to spend in contemplating and nurturing my dream.

How exciting that my fragile dream was taking form, though I was not aware of its power. Ever so often I felt that rush of excitement when asked to "lead" in PTA, Scouts, and various community projects. I realized these peak experiences were part of my dream.

Opportunity came in those days all wrapped up in hard work for others. As every mother knows the myriad of details in running a home often engulf even our private thoughts. But inside each of us is an indomitable struggle for survival that does not stay buried. It continues to smolder until it ignites us to meet every challenge with a triumphant spirit. For me the quiet years spent mothering allowed that struggle to grow and become defined.

After years of being recognized only for my domestic expertise, opportunity knocked again and I took another step toward my dream. The opening of a beautiful Community Civic Center in our town provided me with the opportunity to volunteer for some hard work and valuable experience. I said I would do "anything" and was assigned "everything." Persistent effort paid off again and I was soon the "salaried" Director of Women's Activities.

When our family moved to another state it was through contacts at the Civic Center that I accepted the challenge to introduce a new company and cosmetic to the women of Iowa. The previous experiences of selling and working with women opened the door for another adventure. All I had to do was make a decision to step through. An unbelievable opportunity for personal and financial growth was handed me the day I dreamed I could be the first company Director for that cosmetic line in my state. When I informed the world of my career intents, the comments were almost entirely negative. From questioning the validity of the company and my ability to sell, to my qualifications for motherhood, friends and relatives tried to dissuade me. But the crowning opposition came from an unexpected source, my husband's Board of Directors. They sent a perfectly lovely lady to inform me that my husband's position was such that I should be a "lady of leisure." I will ever be thankful for her visit. Little did they know, even though I smiled sweetly, I was hopping mad! At that point my dream of a successful career became powered by, "I'll show them!" It was not easy to start a new career in a new town where literally everyone was a stranger. Nor was it without much pain that I introduced a brand new product to hundreds of women throughout Iowa. Many of the pains were "growing," as I made countless mistakes in learning my business.

Because I had the stubborn determination to prove myself I worked hard and became first Director in the state. By mentally picturing myself in that position it became physically possible to achieve my dream.

You can have that very thing you dream of if you just plug into the reality of *believing you can*. It is no different for you than for me. The work of this world does not wait to be done by perfect people. Reality is accepting the responsibility to stop all our unproductive habits and start to do the things that make us successful. Making a decision to accept unknown challenges can be the first step in believing your dream will come true. These challenges prepare you for any opportunity that will surely come your way.

Preparation for success had been in the works for thirty years in my life. From selling greeting cards, cupcakes, and soda pop, to teaching aerobic exercises, rearing children and leading other women to success in the glamorous world of cosmetics, I had dreamed big dreams and sold them to others.

Having climbed my mountains, I was still vaguely discontented with my life. My inner needs were not satisfied, my strength not sufficient for my problems. I had nearly grown children, a beautiful home, a successful and handsome husband, freedom to pursue an exciting career—and still I was in quest of the "good life." I began a conscious search for a meaningful life. I did not need to search long, for the God of my childhood soon called me into a new life with Him. Here I found freedom to love with an open heart, freedom from sin and fear, a liberation no politics could decree, and strength to meet all my needs.

And now a whole new world is mine; a dream coming true. I Corinthians 3:21 says, ". . . for all things are yours . . ." In Mark 11:24 I am promised that "What things soever ye desire, when ye pray, believe that ye receive them and ye shall have them."

All the times of my life were my Master's plan to bring me to this point and prepare me for the future. My beginnings have allowed me to open the door of a new firm, *Genesis Point,* permitting us to help guide others from *dreaming and scheming* to *achieving and coping.*

I am assured now "that I can do all things through Christ who strengthens me." Armed with this knowledge I can go forth sharing my talents and my love with you when we meet. I could not do less because I dream of a wonder-filled future for everyone every day.

It is pertinent to base our lives on doing our part, being our best and giving our utmost. Knowing that we reap what we sow, each act of living is a significant expenditure of self. We have the fact and form of life today, but tomorrow is a vision waiting to be claimed.

I would encourage you to design a dream. It is imperative that you construct that dream to fit your personal goals. Give your dream lots of room to develop; one dream on another until you finally find you are striding forth in pursuit of that vision that inspires and motivates you to action.

If you lack a dream, go in search of one. Perhaps covered with the dust of discouragement, and sending out only a glimmer of hope, your dream lies in the attic of your mind waiting for you to expand it into unlimited opportunities. Laying hold of our dream makes it less easy to spend ourselves in meaningless or destructive activity.

When you pursue your dream, you are believing in your eternity. It is in this fact we discover the responsibility of making a dream come true. Assume you are sufficient for your dream! Believe in yourself and you will give wings to your spirit. Without my hopes and dreams my spirit would die and so might yours!

Commitment to your dream calls forth persistence. The pattern of my life became established those early years in such a way that I am still knocking on doors. Life offers challenges daily, but you can only step through *open* doors. Persistence toward a dream and the daily commitment of hard work can unleash our potential and open doors of opportunity. What we have done on our way is history—what we will do as we remain faithful to our dream is our potential.

After choosing what part we must play in reaching our dreams, it becomes necessary to be true to ourselves. To do less than our utmost would be a destructive force turned inward. It is in living every moment fully that we capture the imagination of others and live in grace with ourselves. *Visions become realities* under these conditions.

It is, in the final analysis, our personal performance that creates the "Open Sesame" to our dreams come true. You and I have at our disposal, to use or misuse, a whole lifetime of experiences. But bitter yesterdays can build a wall preventing us from breaking out into a bright and exciting today. Walls of fearful tomorrows keep us isolated from other people and events that provide opportunity and growth. The moment we choose to remove those stones of fear and prejudice, we can scale the wall, opening our hearts to a new vision. Every day becomes a valuable commodity because this day will be spent on the brink of tomorrow.

The opportunity to work with so many women has been proof to me that a pearl of potentiality lives within us, no matter our circumstances at the moment. Every woman I have met can open her opportunity door just as I did. It is no secret. We must, each one, realize our responsibility to generate energy that will fire that dream, allowing our pearl to become a polished reality.

The rich glow of achievement we entertain in our most cherished dreams can only be a product of success qualities polished daily. The words so often quoted, "What you use, you lose," never rings more true than when we neglect to do the things that helped us achieve any success up to this point. Practicing not only sharpens a skill, but helps create new energy and expertise.

Each field has its own jargon and required skills. The list for your business is different than mine. However, common to every endeavor, basic to every dream, are three qualities you each hold now. Hone the skills and all the other rules for success will fall into place.

The first quality you must possess in abundance is your *willingness to work.* Your dream is personal. It is part of you. Therefore your mental and physical senses react when you are contemplating a goal. Your eyes widen, your heart quickens, your mind starts creating, picturing you already in possession of the very thing you want most.

But there will come that day, although the dream survives, that you feel less excited, less creative. It is on this day—and every day like it—that you must make a conscious decision to continue working. To fail to reach your goal because of your own laziness will produce gigantic waves of guilt that could easily inundate your self confidence.

When you have believed and committed yourself to your dream then the only vehicle that will bring you to your destination is to "Keep On Keeping On." Plain old fashioned hard work, the kind that simply gets up in the morning and does the job at hand, will daily renew self-confidence and bring you closer to your goal.

After you have purposely determined to couple your dream with the reality of continued effort be sure to *learn the basics*. Chances are your dream is an extension or offshoot of your present position. Maybe you want to be the boss. Or, if your dream is to try something entirely new, be sure you have a working knowledge of the fundamentals your business is built on. It is a precarious position indeed to climb to the top of any pile without understanding what holds you up. Your dreams of glory may be very real and ever present, but self-confidence and, ultimately, respect for your position, comes from "knowing" your job.

Earlier I wrote to you of the importance of a personal dream and the belief and commitment you must make to your goal. Now we see that to work hard and understand what is required will help make your dreams become realities.

But there is another important, yet intangible, quality, and I believe it is the ability to *relate to and believe in others*. The development of your potential lies in your hands but you need the cooperation of people to reach your dream.

Whether your position requires you deal with customers, employees, clients, your family, kings or cabbages, remember first the Golden Rule. Sincerely strive to treat every person you are dealing with in such a way that they will desire to return your kindness.

This statement raises eyebrows because of our natural wariness of being "taken advantage of." But you see, if your dream is indelibly written on your heart, if you have put that committed effort behind it, you will "to your own self be true." With your eye on the goal, you are not easily side-tracked. Your commitment gives knowledge and strength not only to carry out a dream, but to "do it right." Inside there is a consciousness that will become your witness to truth and integrity if you but listen. This "right" understanding will free you to be open to others, to praise them, to do good by them, to believe, trust, and care for everyone you meet.

Cultivating a giving attitude in all your relationships will create about you a climate conducive to your growth. Good and faithful service to others will pay off in mighty rewards. As you freely give, it will be given back to you. Unburdened by pettiness and trivia, your potential will know no bounds. *Your dream will come true.*

Bettie Kanelos
11842 Hamden Place
Santa Fe Springs, CA 90670
(213) 949-8466

BETTIE KANELOS

Positive thinking and action are things Bettie Kanelos learned early in life. She met every childhood disaster with the outlook that it was meant to strengthen her. In school she set the pace for her classmates, and was involved in many school activities.

Bettie was married to Nick Agosta, and had four fine sons. During the early years of raising her family she spent time each day thinking of methods to better their way of life. While the children were still young she was introduced to the world of Direct Selling, and thus her career began.

To be involved in Direct Sales one must be a self-starter, be ambitious, a positive thinker and have a never-ending well of desire. Most of all, one must know the value of personal goal-setting. All these things were "right up Bettie's alley." She began as a Consultant (saleswoman) with a company that went out of business. But Bettie knew the opportunity in Direct Sales, and set out to find another company.

After locating one she felt could offer the opportunity she sought, she began again. Bettie rose to the top sales status in short order. After achieving her goals as a Consultant, she took her first step up the ladder of success and became a Manager. It was no surprise to those who saw her relate her positive attitude to others that she became the number one National Manager. Bettie then became a Distributor. It was about this time, after a disagreement with the company management, that Bettie was fired, but she caught a new Pearl of Potentiality.

She set out to find a manufacturer. She put together her own line of merchandise with Maurice Cattani whose factory had 25 years of experience. Cattani is the perfect "marriage" of manufacturing and marketing.

Bettie began the 'Prima/Cattani of California' business with only 17 saleswomen. Thirteen years later Bettie and her entire family with her large National Sales Staff produce several million in annual sales.

Today Bettie is still involved in all phases of her business. She would have it no other way. Because of her positive way of life she has earned a beautiful family home and two vacation homes, one at the beach and the other at a lake, plus an assortment of minks and diamonds which she wears like trophies.

The achievement Bettie is most proud of is the fact that the people associated with Prima/Cattani are also successful, and if their goals are material objects, they can earn them.

Rooted within oneself is the source of all influence. Without effort or intent, by our inner attitude we move those of like spirit. To voice a feeling truthfully, to express a sentiment in clear action exerts a mysterious and far reaching influence.
TAO

MARSHMALLOW MAGIC

by Bettie Kanelos

My favorite people are the ones with desires. If they have dreams and desires, I can teach them everything else. I am a teacher of achievement. I have helped people from every walk of life, even some who have been in prison. With a burning desire, a positive attitude, and a set goal, I believe everyone can catch that pearl. I guess I have always had a burning desire to make money. Even as a youngster in Texas, I would beg my mother to go with me to the pecan bottom near our small farm house to pick up the bones of dead animals, for then my dad would take them to town, sell them for me and I could make money. I had a desire as a child to be so rich some day that I could buy all the fluffy marshmallows I could eat. To this day, when I pass a marshmallow counter, I pause, sniff, and smile to myself, for I have learned how to achieve that dream, and countless more!

I have reached every personal goal I have set for myself. A custom-built home in the most prestigious area in Downey, California. A waterfront home at a private lake. And my favorite, a small beach house at a private beach. All the fine jewelry I want. Several fur coats. And I drive the car I desire. Most of all, I'm surrounded by successful happy people, all reaching their goals through the company I have devoted much of my life to. The biggest goal of all I have always had was to have my sons proud of me. Much of my time during their growing-up years was divided between them and business. This often bothered me. I so often wondered, "What do they really think of me as a mother?" Until several weeks ago I wasn't quite sure I had reached this goal. We were just ending a very successful manager's conference, and I gave a speech and in it mentioned "What part of your life are you willing to give up for success?" I wondered if my sons felt I had shorted them on their childhood. At the end of my speech and a standing ovation from the crowd, my three sons, one at a time came up, Nick first, and said, "You are really something"; Aaron next, "I love you"; Rick next, "I am so proud of you."

Story of Bettie Kennard Kanelos

Born Bettie Jean Kennard, June 22, 1931 in Glen Rose, Texas, I was the last of five children, four girls and one boy. We were all born several years apart. By the time I was ten years old, there was only my one sister and me left at home. The others had moved to California. My oldest sister has passed away and then, just two months later, my father died, leaving my mother with no means of support. My brother and sister came to Texas for the funeral and took us to live in Los Angeles.

My mother had never worked before and the only thing she could do was domestic work. We always had to live with either my brother or my sister, not having a home of our own. At this point in my life, I knew I had to go to work as soon as I could. I would not ask my mother for the things I knew she could not afford.

My first job was at the age of twelve, working for a friend in a restaurant during lunch hours for 25¢. It would end up as 50¢ since a nice man always left me a 25¢ tip each day. During junior high and high school, I worked weekends and summer vacations at two places: a 5 & 10¢ store and an ice cream store. Whichever place needed me, I worked. I always earned enough money to buy my own school clothes.

I graduated from John C. Fremont High School in 1949 and shortly thereafter married Nick Agosta, the father of my sons, my business partner, and my best friend, even though we have been divorced since 1970.

Back in 1951, Nick and I bought a cute tract home shortly before our first son, Nick Jr., was born. Three years later came Aaron. Three years later came Ricky. And two years later came Brent. During these early years of marriage and having babies, I constantly sought ways of making money, sewing a little and ironing for some of my working neighbors. I even managed a group of paper boys. All these things I could do from home. That was the only way I could work, as our youngest son Brent was born with brain damage and could not be left alone because of convulsions. After about three years of constant care of Brent, our very dear friend and doctor said, "Young lady, you must do something for yourself." His suggestion was party-plan. This meant I could be home during the day and be gone just a couple of hours in the evening a few days a week while Nick baby-sat. God only knew we could use the extra money, as every dime Nick made had a place to go.

I took a lingerie kit out for almost $300 with a local lingerie company and started putting on home fashion shows. I loved it, but the company wasn't doing well and decided to become distributors for another lingerie company. This meant buying another sample kit, and I did. I couldn't stop now. The pearl had been thrown to me and I could not lose it. I became a manager and won a trip to Hawaii which I couldn't take because of my little boy's condition. But I had done so well I was offered a franchise at the cost of $2,500. This I didn't have. But we had just paid our car off, so off to the bank I went and borrowed as much as I could, and a very good friend loaned me $1,000. Within two years, I became their largest distributor and won every prize they offered, including a new Thunderbird.

During this time of building a business, I also lost my youngest son. Brent had taught us patience and love for each other in his four years. No other troubles have ever stopped us, having lived through these difficult times with Brent, then facing his loss together.

I worked for the lingerie company for three years, but was terminated due to several disagreements on policy. Here I was with many good, loyal consultants and friends who had faith in me and believed in the things I stood for. I had to do something for them and, of course, for myself, for I can honestly say, since the first day I bought my first lingerie kit, I have never been broke again.

The one thing I knew best was how to treat people, and in management, especially in direct sales, you are in the people business. People make a company. It does not matter what color they are, the language they speak, or their religious beliefs. We are all people created equal, and I will always be a fighter to see that the guy that does the job best gets the rewards.

I had been fired in July 1967 and by September, in just two months, Maurice Cattani, Nick and I put together a line of exquisite lingerie called "Cattani of California/ Prima." Cattani does the manufacturing and Nick and I do the marketing. The pearl has now become a string of pearls. We are now in our thirteenth year and the company and its people have all grown. We started expanding nationally last year and are in approximately fifteen states today.

Reading this, it might all sound easy. It is, if you enjoy what you do. There have been many times when to drop the pearl would have been far easier, for there are many heartbreaks in business, as in life. The people you trust the most sometimes break you heart. Or you have to fire someone you love dearly. It's all a part of the business world. You have to have heart, but also have to be capable of making decisions that are best for the company, for the company is many people.

How To Be a Successful Manager

In order to be a very successful manager, you must have or strive to have these very special traits:

1. A desire to help others.
2. Be a likable person.
3. Able to attract other people.
4. Good consistent personal sales.
5. A personality that others want to emulate.
6. You must have the desire to become a leader. It takes patience, understanding, and a willingness to give of yourself.

How To Be Successful in Direct Sales

1. Be Well Dressed.

   Your people will want to emulate you, so if you dress like a business person your Sales People will do the same. If you and your people dress like business people, you will conduct yourselves in a more businesslike manner.

2. Be On Time.

   As a Manager, it is very important that you attend all company functions punctually. For example: if you have a new recruit coming to her first meeting, and she walks into a room full of strangers, and you have not arrived, she will withdraw into a shell and it will take you twice as long to get her into the full outgoing swing of things. If you would have been there on time you could have introduced her to everyone and she would have felt at home right away.

3. Be Positive.

You must have a positive attitude at all times. If your Sales People come to you with a negative situation, and you meet this situation in a positive manner, it will seem of less importance to her by the time you are finished with the conversation. If you meet the situation in her same negative manner, the situation will become blown way out of proportion.

4. Be a Pacesetter.

You, as the Manager, are also the leader. Your people under you will follow the pace set by you. You cannot ask people to do something you are not willing to do yourself. If you want them to do all the things that will make them good Sales People, you must first do them yourself.

5. Be Company-Minded.

Being company-minded is nothing more than backing the company in all promotions and functions. If the company runs a promotion or has a function, it is not always "just right" for everybody. It is up to you as the Manager to push for 100% participation by all your people, and do this with a very positive attitude.

6. Be a Goal Setter.

We are firm believers in setting goals. However, we believe you should set goals that are attainable. If you set goals that are too difficult, you will become depressed when you do not achieve them. By setting goals you feel a great pride of accomplishment when they are reached and can move on to a higher goal. You as a Manager, should have goals.

7. Be Organized.

In order to work at your highest capacity you must set yourself a time schedule. If you don't, you end up thinking about work 24 hours a day, actually working two, and being totally exhausted.

If you break your days down into morning and afternoon activities—put them on a calendar, get up and get them done—you will end each day in a completely different frame of mind—believe me, it feels good to know you did not leave anything for tomorrow.

If you invest 20 well-spent hours a week in your work, you will be a success. While setting your time schedule always remember one thing, and keep this little letter game in mind:

—W W W W W W — Work Will Win, Where Wishing Won't!

Our goals have all been reached, for not only are my sons and co-workers proud of *me,* it is very mutual, as I am equally proud of them. All three of my sons are in the business with their father and me and doing a fine job. They share the love of the business. And when I say "business" I mean the people. I think they too have a hold on that pearl. Won't you join me and catch a pearl of your own. Whatever your dreams or desires are, they are *possible.* Set yourself a goal and go after it. Success can be yours, and yours, and yours. Look up, the air is full of Pearls of Potentiality!

Ruth Arent, M.A., M.S.C.
5800 E. Stanford Ave.
Englewood, CO 80111
(303) 771-4437

RUTH ARENT

Ruth Arent has a wonderful time as a national speaker, an educator and a therapist. She tells how this combination of professional skills have become bundled together. As a child, things were bleak, but gradually she discovered the potential in her pocket. She urges you to understand that everyone has barriers to overcome but the pearls of potentiality are ever present to be discovered and polished.

Mrs. Arent is a graduate of Skidmore College and did her professional training at the State University of Iowa and the University of Denver School of Social Work. She continues to teach a variety of graduate courses dealing with emotionally disturbed children as well as gifted and talented students. She has published a book and two unique wall-charts for schools in these same areas. The topics of her speeches vary from Learning to Trust is a Private Affair, to Family Violence—No Longer a Taboo Topic, to Caring, Coping and Accountability, a Perplexing Problem. All of them provide a challenging way for Ruth to fulfill her potential as a professional in the helping arts.

She is the mother of four children, one is an acupuncturist, one an artist, a third girl is planning to go to medical school and a son who is an engineering student.

Seeded in all small things is the possibility of all great things.
TAO

POTENTIAL IN YOUR POCKET

by Ruth Arent

I am in the People Business. I love doing what I do. Why? Because I sleep better at night knowing that someone may be helped as a result of what I have shared this day.

I am a professional speaker. I am a therapist, a teacher, a social worker, consultant and author. More important, I am a wife, a mother, a friend, a woman . . . a person who cares about other people. All of these dimensions are bundled together to determine why I do what I do.

Potential

I never dreamed I had any! As a child I did not know I had potential in my pocket. Over the years I have discovered the Pearls in my pocket and have become confident. My confidence developed as a result of a combination of hard work and a philosophy of how to be a helper in a variety of ways. A working philosophy is an important basis from which to venture into anything you really want to do.

I was an unwanted child—a mistake. It was not unusual for me to be told, "I never wanted any more children and certainly not a *girl!*" I picked up the message that girls are like leftovers, sometimes useful, seldom outstanding and with limited potential. When my parents divorced I was seven. It was announced to me that neither of them wanted me. I lived with my father by default. A sense of loneliness was implanted. This sense of loneliness has had great power over my life. I felt alienated from adults—hurt and afraid. This alienation from adults was a significant barrier to my realization that I had all kinds of potential. At school I became an underachiever. In a swimming pool I became a champion and that was my only opportunity to feel competent as a young person.

It is not surprising that my goals evolved at an early age. I wanted to be effective in keeping others from suffering as I had suffered. I wanted to go into the People Business. I believed that as a nursery school teacher I could give small children the experience of a trust relationship with an adult. This would provide each one with the strength to overcome whatever problems he might have to confront. Whatever age you may be, it is so invigorating to set goals, so reinforcing to achieve them one by one.

It became apparent to me as time went on, that in the classroom there were a few children whom I could not reach. This determined my decision to become a graduate psychologist with an emphasis on child development. Further work in adoptions and with infants in institutions necessitated more professional training in the art of being an effective therapist. I was putting my philosophy to work ... seeking the potential in every patient and attempting to find appropriate ways for them to appreciate such potential and use it. *Two problems were fundamental to all barriers and maladaptive behaviors . . . two problems really got in the way . . .*

Learn to Trust

The patient had never learned to trust and the patient had never learned the extent to which he or she could be responsible for his or her emotions, choices, and fulfillment. The fears and the anger seemed overwhelming—in the youngest of children and in the sophisticated adults as well. You may have experienced times in your life when barriers seemed unsurmountable and when you have lost sight of your strengths and your talents. Hopefully, someone gave you a boost, as I endeavor to assist others who may have started out in life with the cards seemingly stacked against them. No matter how high the barriers may be, or profound the problems, the potential in the pocket is not destroyed.

I wanted to widen my horizons, work with more people. As a therapist I was limited. I wanted to go beyond the one-to-one work of the office. There were simply too many children and adults, too many families needing service. From a base of a mental health center or a school district, I instituted programs for parents, Big-Brother, Big-Sister regimes in schools, and developed workshops and seminars for educators, parents, students and the community at large. I tackled the tender, taboo topics such as suicides, single parent problems, family violence as well as the more popular concerns of child development, the drug scene, motivation and personal growth. The more speaking that I did, the more I realized that the platform is a special place from which to perform social services!

Helping Arts

Can you imagine how it feels to be asked to talk about sensitive areas such as child abuse, wife battering or suicide to a group of 400 people at a businessmen's convention? That is hardly the standard entertainment bill of fare! Please be reassured that it is possible to handle such timely and important topics *without threatening the audience or pointing a finger at anyone.* It adds a special dimension to the helping arts.

It is no secret that many adults hurt inside because of a history of painful events. They may feel undernourished or unnurtured. Many of them are involved in unhappy relationships. Yet they shy away from services or help which necessitates appointments, interviews and interruptions of work schedules. These same persons do want to be informed and may readily welcome useful ideas. A man might be in an audience and hear it said, "Wife beating occurs even in the loveliest of neighborhoods," and the statement, backed by reasons and a *how-to-get-help* discussion may offer the listener the needed boost to go forth and change his behavior. Words from the podium are far enough away to provide distance—and near enough to provide encouragement.

Most convention speeches are geared to a "Go-Go, Knock 'em Dead" flavor. These are exciting to do some of the time. At other times I enjoy reaching into the problems that keep people from fulfillment. Rather than build up the roller coaster peak of the sales curve, I share ideas about the anxieties and problems which may get in the way. In whatever work that you may do, it is important to consider the weighty with the light, the superficial with the profound, the myriad of levels which add to your competency and the challenge of the job.

Become a Speaker Too?

You may want to join the ranks of microphone enthusiasts. Do select a nucleus of areas that you want to weave into your talks. You can be a generalist or a specialist. I always weave in the areas of trust and responsibility and the companion dimensions of confidentiality, fun, aliveness, caring and coping. Then I give examples . . . again and again and again . . . it is great sport. It is fun for me and fun for the audience and will be fun for you. Examples show that you have been there . . . that you are authentic, that you have done your homework. Add personal experiences, mix generously with smiles, humor, specific *how to* suggestions and encouragement and you will feel as if your pearl is really polished!

We are all designed as multi-faceted persons. When potential in one area is utilized, offshoots in other areas may be expected. This has been my experience. I expanded writing—both a book and educational materials. Echoing the pattern of progressing from individual to group, from clinic and classroom to the large audience, so too I wanted to help the greatest number of special students in the most expeditious way possible. I developed two wall charts (one with an associate), one to identify learning disabled children and the other the gifted, creative and talented. Each chart tells how to work with these students and ways to measure successes. *One* chart posted in a school can dramatically affect the learning program for *many* children. A helping tool indeed. Happily, the charts now adorn the walls of schools in every state, New Zealand, England, Guam and Holland.

My book entitled *Teaching Through Trust, Success with Reluctant Learners* describes a step-by-step method for helping unhappy students learn to feel safe with adults. *It is acknowledged that trust is the antecedent of all learning.* This book tells the story of three boys who had never learned to trust and what school procedures were effective in working with them. In a sense, it represents the marriage of the classroom and the clinic, couched in a story that adults find interesting and worthwhile. Only after teaching teachers all over the country for more than seven years did my experiences and ideas crystallize into book form. Each task had served as a rehearsal for this new product from potential. I urge you to see each task that you do as contributing to the development of the pearl which nestles in your pocket.

You may have already discovered that you can manage being the head of a household and a professional at the same time. I don't know how one measures one's potential as a father or as a mother. I only know that my dreams of motherhood covered those areas of omission that had so affected my early life; omissions such as companionship, nurturing of talents and above all, expressions of love. Throughout my professional phases, I maintained a non-negotiable position—my children were entitled to the same considerations that my patients, my clients and my audiences enjoyed. Their father had passed away. It was inevitable that I had to confront the problems of the single parent, adolescents, young adults and demothering. In effect, as family patterns shifted, I was experiencing new ways to depend on my potential to see me through! It certainly added spice to the People Business.

The conflict between traveling and having kids at home had been painful. The children would vacillate. But one thing was patently clear to all of us . . . travel meant bread. I shared my work with the children as far as possible. They would accompany me on trips, attend presentations, listen to my tapes and edit articles that I wrote. "Mother, that is *not* English," my son would exclaim, following the teachings of an expository writing course. One daughter designs my overheads, brochures, handouts and illustrated *Teaching Through Trust*. Her calligraphy is beautiful.

Finally, the children were understanding about my anxiety when I decided to forego a guaranteed yearly wage and become an independent contractor. I could never go back to the nine-to-five security system. I harbor a need to grow, discover new potential and become even more proficient in doing what I do. This is very exciting. You will find that this excitement as a challenge of the future, approached with the talents of today, is the hallmark of the professional.

One is not born a Superstar. With potential in your pocket, create your philosophy, pursue your goals, enjoy your confidence, and diversify . . . Please, please Polish your Pearls!

Pamela Grein
1334 Lincoln Avenue
San Jose, CA 95125
(408) 289-8313

PAMELA GREIN

Born in Iowa, Pamela Grein grew up in Southern California where competition is a way of life. Her father, an elementary school principal, taught her to tackle nothing half-heartedly. Her mother showed her to fight for right and not to give up. Married in 1977 to Forrest Grein, a product manager for Tandem Computers, Pam is now 35 and has a daughter, Krista 14, and son Donald 10.

Pam does not look like your typical high powered business woman. Her actions and dress reveal her as a homemaker and these are the people she relates to in her business. A room mother, Home and School Club Board Member, Christian Women's Club Board Member and an active participant in her husband's activities at work, help her understand the women she deals with.

With her background of Tupperware, Vanda Beauty Counselor, Dart Industries, and Act II Jewelry, she founded Daisy Fashion Jewelry in 1975.

When first asked to write this chapter, Pam dismissed the idea as too monumental to undertake in such a short period of time, having never written anything before. However, when Dottie Walters persisted, even after a second "no," going so far as to inconvenience herself, Pam realized that God's hand was at work. She asked friends, relatives and God for ideas. The story first came together on a baseball field, where she wrote most of the story on a cardboard box she had with her. The words flowed . . . God's work. The next day sitting down to put it all together she received a call from a top area manager in Utah who said she had listed eight points about Pam that she felt explained Daisy's success. The points summarized the chapter. God's work again!

This chapter was meant to be. It's Pam's story, but it was written with prayer!

20

Unity without a central influence emanating from a common Inner Truth is a deceptive fabrication. When commanding a situation the strength of one's personality must be so strong that its suggestion effects the unity of all adherents.

TAO

A LIFE SO FULL . . . IT OVERFLOWS!

by Pamela Grein

The sound of music and applause fills the room as the people stand and applaud the woman trying to make her way to the front of the room. She is stopped at every table with hugs and tears and congratulations. I stand at the podium with tears in my eyes and I feel successful. I know that this is what Daisy Fashion Jewelry is all about. It is not the product we sell, our jewelry, it is that woman and all that this award she has just received means. The award, "Bouquets To You," a recognition of personal growth. Judy, the recipient, was so sure two years ago that she was no one special. A housewife with small children, she didn't realize the talent and love she had stored up inside her to give. This was God's purpose for Daisy. A vehicle to help people realize their potential. A way to touch lives and give them fullness. How very special I feel to be a part of this plan to help people reach for their dreams.

Pam Pixies

My education was all directed toward my plans to be a teacher. Then a special lady shared her career story, her opportunity with me and I started selling a product, part-time at Home Parties. Two months later, totally in love with direct selling and its special people, I was standing in front of my Distributor's warehouse on a bright and beautiful Monday morning with the keys to a "brand new" Company car in my hand! My dealers and I were so proud to be promoted to our own unit . . . "Pam Pixies." I was their Manager! I am so thankful to that Manager and Distributor who looked at me and saw beyond age and lack of training. They saw "potential" and made me feel extra special. One of the Company Vice Presidents from Florida attended that assembly. He smiled at me when he was giving his speech and after the meeting, told me I was the youngest Manager in the country! Whether I was or not really didn't matter, because I felt "super neat"!

That was the 1st new car anyone in our family ever had. I could hardly wait to arrive in front of my Mom's house that morning and see her excitement! "Head over heels" in love with a business that didn't care that you were a woman, or that you were nineteen years of age, I decided this would be my career. I would make every effort to share this opportunity with everyone who would listen.

Be Special!

Surround yourself with people who make you feel special. If your life is filled with negatives, you'll never realize your potential. If you are working right now in a situation that makes you feel like a number . . . *get out!* You have to feel special to be special.

My family made me feel special, they helped me grow. We were not financially "well off" but my parents provided a beautiful life with what they had. As a little child we moved every year, at least once, until I was about ten. Through this experience I learned to make new friendships — quickly! I learned that people were more important than possessions. My confidence came from my Grandfather. He would tell me that I could sell anything! He would say, "with your smile, how can anyone resist?" It didn't matter that I was pudgy or had a crooked tooth, he said I was beautiful, so I was! He sent for Christmas cards and stationery and sent me out "door to door." When I returned home he listened to my story and regardless of the results, he praised my efforts. A little praise can erase most problems. I was ready to go again.

He entered me in a race at a company picnic once and I won a beautiful doll. As a teenager, I reminded him of that day. He laughed and told me that because I was so tiny, he had entered me in a race with children one year younger. I said that wasn't fair. He said he knew, but — "You are a winner, and I wanted you to realize it!" A beautiful man, not successful as the world would judge, he never earned large sums of money, but even though his formal education ended in sixth grade, he could intelligently discuss subjects like medicine, atomic fusion and the sciences. A man of vision, I thought him very successful.

People to Love

My direct selling career began to take shape. A warehousing distributor first for a cosmetic company and then a jewelry party plan gave me the experience I needed with people. I learned to work with all types of people from different backgrounds and found things I could love about each one. First impressions shouldn't be lasting! I learned to look beyond what I saw on first encounter, whether good or bad, and looked at the person's dream. If they didn't have one, major surgery was needed! It became clear that most women didn't think much of themselves. You will be amazed at the things that will happen in your life when you help someone look inside themselves and find all their talent they aren't aware of!

The special beauty of party plan selling is that it allows you the best of both worlds. Homemaker, mother, and career woman!

Working as an Area Manager on the staff of one of Dart Industries subsidiary companies was exciting! During that time, working with couples who were all building their own businesses in different ways, I gained ideas that I would use in later years to plan my Daisy Company.

There are things in some party plans that I didn't enjoy doing and things I loved, and so when the plans for Daisy were formulated I tried to think like a dealer when planning for dealers, and like a manager when setting up our management. I felt that Daisy was a better idea and I was ready to share it!

Ready to Share

I went with my idea in mind to a local jewelry wholesaler in San Jose. I shared my plans and my financial situation, approximately $200 in capital. He laughed, but said if I would put it all up, he would give me credit. Another wholesaler in the area, a woman, thought the idea was fascinating and helped me too. They supplied us with jewelry and I paid as I could. My accounts with them grew, but their faith in Daisy never wavered. They would listen to our "ups" and "downs" and always encouraged me.

My Sister-in-law helped me by holding my first Daisy party. It was a smash ... Over $200 in sales and six datings! For the next year I drove every week night 100 miles round trip to hold parties. Dinner was mostly tacos in the car on the way to parties and many nights I would pull off the freeway into a gas station to sleep for a few hours because I just couldn't make it home. My office manager, Bev Cole, and I did all of the office and warehouse work ourselves. She did all the figuring, packing and shipping, while I dreamed, wrote, and published all of our literature, sales promotion, bulletins, held a weekly sales meeting and trained our new people. We were tired, but it was so exciting and our managers were starting to grow.

As we grew, it was apparent that in order to offer our management a great earning opportunity we would have to buy direct from the manufacturers. We were receiving invitations to go and choose a new jewelry line, but because of my tight financial situation, I didn't feel I could even spare the air fare. Bev and I were in the office one day when her husband, Harry, "dropped by." We talked about Daisy, our plans and dreams and he said that he and Bev had been discussing Daisy at home. He knew that if we were going to make it, I would have to start buying our jewelry from its original source. He and Bev were giving me $1000 from their savings because "we love you and believe in Daisy!" I cried! We hugged and laughed and called for the plane reservation. One week later I was on the plane traveling to the United Jewelry Show. As the plane left the ground, tears on my cheeks . . . "Thank you Lord for Bev and Harry!"

Parting

Making your own decisions, without prayer . . . wow, what a heartache! I personally don't like the song "My Way." A little guidance and prayer can save you and others a lot of harm. My largest trial was marital problems. First divorcing a man whose only fault was having married a woman who was not committed to him. Lots of patient understanding allowed us to part friends and have two spectacular children . . . everything happens for a reason! A second divorce for me was devastating! How could this happen to me—now? *Easy!* My own decisions, against God's will! Now on my knees . . . "Oh Lord, it is obvious I can't do this 'my way.' Please take hold of my personal life . . . Guide me!"

One thought I have come to know as fact, like the lesson of the prodigal son, God's love is tenacious! With every stumble, each time I did things "my way," the understanding touch of a patient God helped me get up! Time and again, blessings and more blessings.

Each event in your life has a purpose and I know that when I was four years old and my mother remarried, my new father was God's choice for me. His love over the years made me see how God's love works. He chose me for his child and showed me right from wrong. He was upset and disappointed when I made mistakes, but his love and forgiveness was always there. Like a good father, God's love is always there.

I was sure God loved me because even with my mistakes, He kept blessing me: good health, my daughter Krista, son Donald, parents, relatives and friends that loved me and made me feel special. I wasn't afraid to do things His way!

Give Up?

Oh how the blessings came! I met Forrest Grein when Daisy was a little over a year old. What a special, loving man. I was having heavy financial struggles and many doubts about whether Daisy would make it. My divorce had left me in a super mess with unbelievable debts. My ex-husband had left the state and couldn't be located, so the State Tax Board wanted their money from his car business from me. Attorneys recommended I declare bankruptcy and go "home to Mama." My beautiful Mom said, "What do they know? They obviously don't know you! But, of course, if you want to *give up,* we're always here!" Forrest said, "I don't know much about party plan, but I think we can make it!" We decided to "buy" some time. The next day I went to the bank with stacks of bills totaling seventy-five thousand plus, and my assets . . . Well, I had myself and an accountant who believed in me and my ability. The Bank Manager looked over the situation and shook his head . . . He looked at me and listened to my determination and I walked out of there with $9000, enough to give Daisy time to grow. Praise the Lord for people of vision!

I went to the tax board, told them my story and they put me on monthly payments. I followed up each bill and set up monthly payment schedules. Every person I dealt with was cooperative and understanding. Some payments were small, but a show of good faith. If I couldn't meet the schedules, I called and set up a new plan. It was important not to leave them "hanging" . . . they always knew the situation.

Forrest and I were married a year later and continued to pay our obligations. Daisy continued to build and grow. The following year our sales manager left to start her own company and some of our top people chose to leave too. Back to my knees! I prayed, "Lord I gave you my personal life and you have blessed me so much. Now, you take the rest . . . you take Daisy, you guide my steps, you choose the right people to build this company and we will give you the praise." I waited and was a little surprised that no super-talented, big name party plan people fell out of the sky on me, but I realized that here was where we were to start! He would provide, as we were ready. I opened my eyes and found the special people that were already a part of Daisy . . . people within my reach! Carol Merkley, one of our managers, now our National Sales Manager, a beautiful lady who certainly didn't realize her talent, blossomed! She made up her mind and grew each day and we began to really grow! Our dealers and managers brought forth friends, sisters, cousins and moms and the Daisy family was on its way. One of our managers gave me a poster that hangs in the office, a bouquet of daisies with the caption, "Happiness is the art of making a bouquet of those flowers within reach" . . . Goodard. How true! The daisies in reach began to blossom and as I believed, when the time was right, we were led to new people. New managers that would help us in the growth and in molding our company image. Our little company, then in California, now has dealers in fifteen states!

A company whose commodity is people! A company that helps people realize their fullest potential through confidence and personal growth. A company that will reach out to anyone who will reach out for themselves! An important thing we can teach our children is that they do not have to accept what life deals to them. All they need is a dream and the realization that they must strive toward it!

Forrest and I decided to sell our home to pay off my final obligation, the tax bill. The property had increased in value such that all of the bank loans and tax debt could be met with enough left over for a small down payment on a "dream come true," a small but beautiful home in the mountains above San Jose. However, instead of the $10,000 of taxes owing, the state now added on penalties and interest bringing the debt to $17,000! I pleaded with the local tax board. Although very sympathetic, their hands were tied in red tape.

Confront the Problem

My parents had taught me to fight injustice. When an incident would come up at school or in an organization, my Mom and Dad would take me to the source and show me how to confront the problem and fight until it was solved. And so, I jumped in my car, drove to Sacramento. Pushed my way in to the Chief Tax Collector for the State of California's office and told him my story! He patiently listened, said he admired my strength and spirit. He picked up the phone, dialed the Attorney General's office and they removed the penalty, interest, and accepted my offer to pay the real debt. So, you see, you can even fight city hall!

Apply these points to your life and amaze yourself!

1. *Open Your Mind*
   Have a willingness to learn from the thoughts and opinions of others. Don't close your mind, there is always more than one way to do something. Keep

looking for the best way, even after you are sure you have found it!

2. *Make People Feel Special*
   Look for something unique and special in every person you meet. Don't be locked into first impressions. Accept people as they are, see their special features and believe that as they open themselves up to personal and spiritual growth, they will achieve a special glow.

3. *Give Yourself Away*
   The most successful people, no matter how many people they deal with, take the time to recognize effort, and correct situations. Make the calls, write notes, send gifts, give personal care to recognize and correct. Give a part of yourself to each customer, dealer, manager. Let every life you touch be better for having met you.

4. *Be Assured*
   Open your mind and heart to God and be assured that He will guide your steps. Get away from well meaning friends who "steal" your enthusiasm by telling you how and why it can't be done.

5. *Let Your Light Shine*
   You are unique! Accept it! Be proud of the way you are. Strive each day to improve, but don't be intimidated by other people's standards. I have been trying to get organized for 35 years. I use a listing system that works for me, but I am constantly teased about my messy office. I tell my friends . . . "I can't clutter my life with tidyness!" The truth is that I am getting neater every year, but I refuse to feel inferior in the meantime.

6. *Grow As You Go*
   Don't be afraid to make changes as your life and career grow. A plan that's perfect today may need

improvements next year. Sometimes you may have to be inconvenienced to make other lives easier.

7. *Show Not Tell*

Don't ask anyone to do something you weren't willing to do yourself. Take them to the task. Give them all you have and whether they succeed or fail, you'll feel good about your effort.

You shouldn't feel disappointed when you have spent a lot of time with someone in your business and she gives up before she succeeds. I have spent way more time on people who have given up than on my success stories! Take heart, the time is never lost, your influence will help them somewhere along their life.

8. *Fail? Only If You Quit!*

Why is Daisy an exciting and growing company today? Only one reason . . . we didn't quit. Most people would have stopped along the way. Our country's statistics on business failures in the early years are unbelievable. Talented, intelligent people with bright ideas and great company plans, failing for one reason—leaders who quit! Four years of prayerful determination have brought us to this step toward our dream. Years of sleepless nights conquered because of dedicated people who helped us hang on by tooth and nail . . . because we believe in what we're building!

One thought I would like to stamp in your mind: Don't be beaten by the way things are or the situations that happen to you—even if you have caused them!

Open your heart and your mind and let yourself be used for a good purpose. Don't worry about your wrinkles, bulges, etc. Take the assets you have and set out toward your dream! Determined, prayerful effort brings *a life so full . . . it overflows!*

Nina Harris
108 W. Loma Vista Drive
Tempe, AZ 85282
(602) 968-0231

NINA HARRIS

"One of the advantages of teaching in an elementary school is that you can always find a place to park!" quips former teacher, counselor and administrator, Nina Harris.

Temporarily blinded as a child, Nina's personal experiences contribute to her use of humor coupled with warmth and directness as she empathizes with and educates a wide variety of audiences.

Judged at 24 years old to be the youngest woman to be admitted to the Arizona State University doctoral program in educational administration, Dr. Harris holds four degrees and the directorship of her own consulting firm.

A community college instructor in communications skills, Nina's training programs have spread to various universities and colleges throughout the southwest. Her writing spans a decade of recognition by nationally distributed publications with readership topping the million-person-mark.

Most recognized for her childlike voice, Nina surprises her audiences with humor and "tell-it-like-it-is" assertiveness, gaining her the affectionate Arizona nickname, "Mighty Mouse"!

A difficult enterprise is made easy when it is attended to quickly.
TAO

JUST BECAUSE THINGS GO WRONG IS NO REASON YOU HAVE TO GO WITH THEM!

by Nina Harris

Ever heard the old cliche, "The woman's work that's never done is most likely what she asked her husband to do?" As persons we're constantly surrounded by chuckles and quips eluding to male/female ineptness in communication . . . just look at the wealth of humor revolving around mother-in-laws, beer-drinkin', sofa-snoozin' husbands, and ding-bat women drivers!

"When God created Adam He didn't realize what a *mess* He'd made of things; so He created Eve to clean things up, and we've been *stuck* cleaning up ever since!" Against the mostly-female audience's roar of applause, I, as a participant, pondered . . . *Stuck?* Are we really? Do we as women see ourselves as hapless victims of not only traditional humor but unlimited time demands? Before you wave your hand in wild agreement, consider if just perhaps you are the *product of your own choices* . . .

The Frustrating Thing is That the Key
To Success Doesn't Always Fit
Your Ignition . . .

Sound familiar? Are you one of those persons who has a million things they want to accomplish in life but are constantly waylaid by diapers, or lunch pails, or spouse's wrinked shirts . . . whether it's demands from relatives, loved ones, community or your own piped-in tapes from years back, most of us find ourselves thoroughly bound in traditions of "I should," "I can't," "It'd never work" . . . Fear tapes . . . messages that keep us stuck in nice, secure (sometimes dull and boring) spots . . . and one of the *biggest and best crutches* we use to keep us *stuck* is *time . . .!*

How many times have you heard or commented to yourself, "I'd *love* to do that, but I just *don't have the time.*" Here's another good one, "I'd just give anything to be program chairperson, but the *children need me at home.*" Hmmm . . . How about, "I was so honored to be asked to represent XYZ Corporation at their regional meeting, but George says *no wife of his is going to travel.*" Familiar statements? My hunch is that by the time you've read this far, that perhaps you're feeling resentful or a little angry or discouraged . . . please don't give up reading yet . . . hang in for just a little longer as we explore where these messages come from, and what we can do to get the things *we want in life* and yet still deal effectively with those persons we love.

There Is No Sadder Or More Frequent
Obituary On the Pages of Time Than,
"We Have Always Done It This Way."

As women, we're particularly torn among the roles we've selected to play in life . . . notice the words, "we've selected" . . . you see, many of our choices for our lives came about even before we gave much conscious thought to our *full potential as women* . . . We became sweethearts, and wives, and mothers often without much forethought; when the pursestrings became a little tight, often with reluctant blessings from "George," we became clerks or secretaries or substitute teachers, because after all, this is only temporary. Many of us became "workers until" . . . *until* the mortgage's paid; *until* the braces are paid off; *until* George is well. Even as divorce or death hit our marital doorstep, we blindly stuck to *until* . . . *until* I remarry; *until* the kids are in school; *until* . . . *until*. All of us tend to put off living . . . we dream of some magical rose garden over the horizon instead of enjoying the roses outside our windows today . . .

Dale Carnegie's famous words substantiate the findings of a survey administered by psychologist William Moulton Marston in which 3000 persons were asked what they had to live for . . . *94%* were simply enduring the present while they waited for the future . . . *until* . . . *until* . . . never in touch with the fact that *all they had was today* . . . tomorrow is never a "given" . . .

It Would Be Nice if All Life's Problems Hit At Eighteen, When We Knew Everything!

Remember the bravado we all had when we were young? Remember the dreams? Dancing through the streets of Paris . . . writing the Great American Novel . . . inventing a 'break-through' in scientific research . . . roaming the wilds of Africa . . . as youngsters, we were fearless, but as the realities of living set in, many of us traded adventure for security . . .

If the closest you've come to realizing your dreams is marrying your handsome prince (and for some of us, those princes really *did* turn into proverbial frogs!) and you still have fragments of dreams unrealized, read on . . . you see *it is possible* to keep what you have now and *attain more* . . . Sound intriguing . . . Here are several *time tamer tips* to help your life become more meaningful, more manageable, more positive for you!

Time Tamer Tip #1:
Too Many People
Confuse Bad Management
With Destiny!

Let's assume for the remainder of this chapter that you, the reader, are swamped with tasks to accomplish . . . that you couldn't begin to get everything done if God gave you a 48-hour-day . . . Sound like you? To be honest, that's the profile for most of us who are attempting to juggle families, careers, educational goals, and community involvement . . . *You must begin with the basic assumption that everyone* (from the President of the United States to Aunt Gertrude) *has exactly the same amount of time to work with . . . 24 hours . . . no deviations . . .* So the challenge lies in using that time most wisely . . . and that means setting attainable goals . . . and knowing where your time's going . . . *that means planning time . . .*

"I don't have time to plan!" you cry. There we are back to that old excuse again . . . that's right . . . *excuse* . . . next time you think, "I don't have time," substitute the words, "I choose not to do that," or "It's not important to me right now." Before you get your psychological dander up, consider how we as women were socialized from the time we were very small to become nurturing, caring individuals toward our spouses, our children, our families and friends. If we aren't good time/goal managers, we can find ourselves in the position of giving out *all of our energy to others without replenishing our storehouse . . .*

Sometimes we choose not to take time for ourselves because to do so would make us feel guilty or torn about our obligations. I can remember the first incident in which I became aware of the entire concept of "taking time-outs" . . . a psychologist . . . male . . . suggested that I take time away from my family to not only realize some personal goals, but also to just plain *rest* . . . my initial reaction was one of anger and frustration . . . how could he possibly understand that there were dishes to wash, shirts to iron, schoolpapers to grade for tomorrow's classes? After all, *he* had a wife!

Underneath that anger was a gnawing realization that he was speaking with an element of truth. Digging a little deeper into my hesitant feelings, I came face-to-face with my heritage. You see, I was taught from the time I was small to "do unto others." With Protestant abandon, I tackled self-imposed tasks with defiant energy and all the sad-facedness of the neighborhood martyr. It took many years for me to come to grips with the concept that true Christian charity comes from *choosing* to do things, not doing things because I felt I *had to* . . . I was receiving no joy from doing; I was tired; depressed; and missing the happiness of relaxed, shared time with others. Because I hadn't learned to be good and give to myself, I had a difficult time receiving from others too!

Time Tamer Tip #2:
Besides the Noble Art of Getting
Things Done, There is the Noble Art
Of Leaving Things Undone.
The Wisdom in Life Consists
In the Elimination of Nonessentials.

Are you efficient or effective? Are you working smart or hard? Many women are tremendously *efficient* . . . we zip through detail work with all of the deftness that years of homemaking have taught us, yet we aren't visionaries . . . we haven't practiced the skills of *looking beyond and out* . . . that's right, *out and beyond* all of the clutter of our day-to-day living patterns. *Effective* persons, on the other hand, are discriminating . . . they know what tasks are vital, what tasks to toss out or delegate to another or streamline into a more efficient (and thus *effective!*) method.

I spent a large portion of my married life (and professional life) "putting out fires" and never getting anywhere . . . yet always feeling exhausted without much reward. I hadn't learned to be an effective problem solver. As a case in point, as an ex-home economics instructor, I felt *committed* to do all my own housekeeping which in my value system meant roses in the bathrooms; fresh bread on the table and linens . . . I even had a short stint at ironing sheets and pillowcases! Not only was I always exhausted for my efforts, but my resentment toward my spouse, who seemed to have unlimited time to play golf, tennis, and fly, was growing leaps and bounds. *I didn't have to keep house so meticulously.* I had choices . . . I could allow certain tasks to slide; I could ask his help in doing the work; I could hire a housekeeper. As I hesitantly viewed my alternatives, I came in touch with the *real value* I was tugging with . . . the old tape that *a good wife keeps a good house* . . . That was it! If I gave up these tasks, someway or other, I subconsciously viewed myelf as a *lesser-than wife!* After much agony in decision-making, I chose to have a housekeeper who maintained my values of roses in the baths and nicely-pressed sheets. My home looked as I wanted, and interestingly, my spouse *preferred more relaxed time with me* . . . he'd been saying that all along . . . It's just that I chose not to listen!

Time Tamer Tip #3:
It's A Funny Thing About Life—
If You Refuse To Accept
Anything But The Best,
You Very Often Get It!

Take time to dream . . . every day. Set aside twenty minutes very early in the morning, very late at night, or during your lunch break, to reward yourself with dreaming, envisioning time. Mentally list all of the things you've ever wanted to do; see them happening in your imagination. Don't allow thoughts of childishness or impossibility to enter . . . after all, *you* are in charge, you *choose* your own thoughts . . . Want to be a prima ballerina? See it clearly! Visit the Roman ruins? See it clearly! No dream is too outlandish or ridiculous!

You'll find as you continue your dream time, that certain attainable dreams will just naturally take over . . . you'll be dreaming them clearly and you'll begin to find steps for their attainment . . . It's like a wonderful, magical trick . . . that when you relax and allow your thought to free-flow, that you become your own, most adept problem-solver! As your twenty minutes come to an end each day, mentally review your dream-trip; pat yourself on the back emotionally for giving yourself the time to relax and dream, and make a commitment to dream time tomorrow! After all, if the successful executives of the world allow themselves daily dream time, you owe yourself the same opportunity to plan your future!

Time Tamer Tip #4:
Log It Or Leave It!

Every day for five days, record how you use your time . . . after all, if time is an expendible commodity, before you reorder a batch of minutes, you ought to, as a good manager, have a sense of where and when that last batch of minutes was consumed! The principles for good time usage are the same principles that are applied to grocery stocking; closet inventorying and household budgeting!

Carry a little notebook in your pocket or take an hourly break and note time-wasters. Don't analyze your lists yet! You may discover time-expenders as you go along and be motivated to *change right now* . . . but hold off. Evaluate at the end of five days. As you review, you'll be astounded at all of the tasks you repeated; the extra trips; the steps you missed initially.

Time Tamer Tip #5:
Grab A Task And Gulp
. . . With Amazement!

Just for fun, identify a small task that you perform daily . . . as a hint, I chose applying my cosmetics in the morning — anything routine — something you feel you have "down pat"! Sketch a rough design of the room or area in which you perform the task . . . my design was a crude draft of the bathroom sink and cabinet area . . . then pencil in hand, perform that task as you normally do, but just this once, record, with a line on paper *every move that you make!* My graph of my arm movements resembled a maze of intersecting lines . . .

Some time later on during the day, coffee cup in hand, analyze *how* you could have done that task more efficiently. What steps can you save? Can the task be eliminated altogether? Can someone else perform the task or share in the work? (I found that my cosmetics were not organized in the order that I used them and that many cosmetics could be discarded.)

Time Tamer Tip #6:
Nature Couldn't Make Us Perfect,
So He/She Did The Next Best Thing
. . . He/She Made Us Blind To Our Faults!

That's why, for this Time Tamer Tip, you need one or two best friends as helpers. Gather all of those troublesome tasks . . . the ones that are gobbling up your time; the ones you find yourself repeatedly doing throughout the day; and bundle them up for display at your next koffee klatch. That's right, use your best friends' expertise to help you manage your time! You see, each one of us has areas of talent . . . places where we shine with good management skills. We also have blind spots . . . areas where others can help us reorganize. For example, one of my friends gave me a "ringer" of a Tip for drawer organization. I'm one of those individuals for whom the quip was aptly written, *A family member is exposed to the danger of fall-out every day when they open the hall closet!* I insist on the exterior, table tops, flooring, and furniture of my home being "showcase perfect" yet in the same breath, know that my dresser drawers are literally dangerous. Paulette suggested using shoeboxes to hold undies . . . three neatly in a row—one box for "ho-hummms"; one for "next in line for the ragbag" and one for "Saturday Night Specials"! A terrific tip, one many of you probably use, yet one I was not implementing in my organizational routine.

By the way, our brainstorming sessions resulted in time-managing "fun for us" . . . we found that much as we loved each other, we were five friends that were swamped with work and often *chose* not to make time for each other . . . we'd not visit for weeks at a time . . . So we locked in the first Saturday of every month to rotate koffee klatches. We stay exactly two hours; we share in the refreshments; and we invite new women to the group as we meet them. One of our goals became *maintaining the friendships* we'd established. (I firmly believe that there is nothing adverse to "locking" or "calendaring in" time for visiting, exercising, religion, and romance. We often *choose not to have time for the relaxing activities that are most vital to maintaining our relationships!)*

Time Tamer Tip #7:
A Calendar By Any Other Name . . .

Calendars are crucial to more efficient use of time . . . unfortunately I think many of us don't make the *best use* of our calendars because (a bid for better planning time again!) we don't *choose* the calendar that suits our needs . . . Browse through a stationer's store and get feel for the many types of calendar formats printed. Ask yourself what suits your needs and your lifestyle best . . . what format is the one that you'll be most apt to use? In my particular case, my calendar is 8½″ × 11″ (I carry it either in my attache case or under my attache-shaped purse!); it is expensively-bound (I want a professionally-appearing calendar plus I don't want the hassle of transferring dates midyear when a less-expensive calendar would become dog-earred); it has 15-minute time designations 6 a.m. to 10 p.m. (I work at all and odd hours and I also write horribly . . . I need all of those little lines to keep my writing straight!); and it doesn't have space for separate note, phone and "to do" lists (my style is to cluster different tasks in a time frame so I don't separate tasks out). Your needs may be 180 degrees different from mine, but the point is that you know what those needs are and develop a calendar-keeping program that fits you . . . by the way, the first thing that I log into my calendar is daily time for me . . . *every day* . . . it may be a walk on the beach, a long-distance phone visit with a friend, a glass of wine, a massage, a pedicure, a cookie, or a snooze . . . the time varies each day, but the important thing is that it is there and I use it just for my own rejuvenation!

Time Tamer Tip #8:
A Person Cannot Remake Themselves
Without Suffering, For They Are
Both The Marble And The Sculptor

Be patient and loving with yourself as you strive to remake habits and reset goals. We've all been exposed to so many negative, put-down messages in our growing . . . It's so easy to "buy into" believing that dreams aren't for real, and goals aren't attainable. They are!

Be aware that though this chapter is focusing on our roles as women, that men and children as well have difficulties in 'prioritising,' in saying 'no' to others and 'yes' to themselves at appropriate times. We are "all in this together" as the saying goes!

I love proverbs and sayings that gently and sometimes humorously remind me what my life is about . . . my closing gift to you is a listing of some of my favorites:

*Life is the art of drawing without an eraser.

*Experience should be a guidepost, not a hitching post!

*Before you let yourself go, be sure you can get yourself back.

*To be able to love a butterfly, we must be able to love a few caterpillars.

*Remember these trying times will be the "good old days" in just a few years!

*and — *just because things go wrong is no reason you have to go with them!*

Zonnya Harrington
P.O. Box 2408
New Orleans, LA 90176
(504) 581-4357

ZONNYA HARRINGTON

Zonnya grew up in a small town on a farm in southeast Missouri. Working over 60 hours a week, she put herself through college and graduated in three years.

She accepted a real challenge teaching high school juniors and seniors. For five years, she was committed to preparing young men and women to face a grown-up world. Working in other fields, real-estate, direct selling, professional writer, airline attendant, she learned a lot about people and how each have certain needs that must be fulfilled. As her career moved toward the people business, she began to dream new dreams, set new goals, and work toward them.

Her writing led to many interesting people and experiences. After joining the staff of Bob Harrington, Inc., she was assigned the directing of his radio and T.V., also the editor of a monthly publication. At this point, she began to do speaking on her own.

Recently, Zonnya co-founded and presently directs the Total Living Center, Lakeland, Florida. It is a self-improvement motivatonal center dedicated to helping people fulfill more of their God-given potential in all areas of life: physical, mental, spiritual, financial, and family. Spending time in New Orleans as Executive V.P. of Bob Harrington, Inc., directing the Total Living Center in Lakeland, Florida and speaking in conventions and seminars keeps her life most interestingly filled.

Every day is a new experience with new dreams, and goals, and a plan by which to move toward their reality. The master key that has unlocked doors to fulfillment is that which she shares in all her speaking: healthy self-love; the ability to do her own thinking; the courage to accept her responsibility in this wonderful thing called life.

22

One is strong who conquers others: One who conquers self is mighty.
LAO-TSZE

DO YOUR OWN THINKING—
NOBODY WILL BELIEVE IT!

by Zonnya Harrington

Just imagine a small farming community in southeast Missouri with heavy emphasis on life derived from the "Bible-Belt" philosophy. The men and women of this farm-land area believed and perpetuated the belief that "Success was a Secret" and only a few knew the secret. This setting and philosophy dominated a major portion of my life. Strangely enough as I proceeded my discovery of life, I would meet many men and women who had experienced a similar life style. Our society through every institution — church, home, school, government, business — indicates to us that many of our pursuits in life are wrapped in an "aura of mystique," in other words, a Secret. But as I began my journey on the numerous streets of realistic thinking, I was to learn one of the most important truths that brings life-changing results; that is:

Success is Not a Secret—Success is a System
Happiness is Not a Secret—Happiness is a System
Wealth is Not a Secret—Wealth is a System
Health is Not a Secret—Health is a System
Opportunity is Not a Secret—Opportunity is a
   System

Every rainbow—past, present, future—can be pursued with the philosophy that with a system—*all things are possible.* Every opportunity that we make for our lives can be caught with the determination of developing just the right "system" for turning opportunity into the occasion to pick our peaks.

Think!

To see opportunity and catch the pearl of potentiality, we must be keenly aware of the basic ingredients for this unique insight. As I travel over 100,000 miles each year, speaking to groups, conventions, seminars of all types and sizes, I have become aware of an acute deficiency in the practical, as well as the philosophical, faction of our society. Today we seem to be generating this philosophy: "Beware: Thinking may be hazardous to your health." From birth on through to death, we all have the tendency to let someone else think for us. And once again, every institution that comprises our society perpetuates the concept that someone else will do our thinking. As I grew up in that little farming community of southeast Missouri, no one ever taught me the skills of doing my own thinking. Through the many years of my education, no one ever challenged me to think for myself. Certainly, the school will not further the "think for yourself" concept. If that were taught, teachers would have to be better prepared. Generally speaking, those in our educational system can not tolerate a student who thinks for herself, to challenge the knowledge or lack of knowledge of the leader.

Then, there is the government. They tell us, "Don't worry about it; we'll take care of it for you." Of course, you and I know that when the government says "We'll take care of it for you," we've really got problems. Then, there is the church. Religious leaders will be the last to encourage us to think for ourselves because they might "lose control" and their power and influence might be threatened. Last, but not least, is the institution of the family. Seldom will a husband and wife encourage each other to think individually. Their non-thinking prohibits the mother and father from teaching the children those valuable techniques that make us all so unique. So—here we are: products of the five major institutions that continue to spin the merry-go-round of allowing someone else to think for us.

You Are Special

Now—Today—is the exact time to stop that merry-go-round and develop that system for our own special individual lives. When God created man and woman and they began to populate the earth, God's system said this: "Every individual is created in the image of God with her own special and unique qualities that totally distinguish her from any other creature." The day that I understood my "specialness," my life began to change. I began to see the opportunities that I could create in my life to make my life more valuable. There is no one created with a mind like mine or yours. There is no one created with the same ability and potential that I have or that you have. There is no one created who has the right to impose upon our thinking as we do it for ourselves. The truth of the matter is this: No one can, in fact, think for us unless we give them the opportunity and the power to exercise over us. When I fully realized that I am a "special" person—for I am the only one just like me—I began to live a "special" life. In every area of my life, I began to emphasize my "specialness." I could not believe the transformations that

I began to experience. Remember: *You are a special person, and special persons live special lives!*

Reserve the Right to Think For Yourself

Because we are "special" people, we have a responsibility to make a worthwhile contribution to our world. Every person alive has six areas that combine to make up her world. They are: physical, mental, spiritual, social, financial, and family. In all six of these areas, on a day-to-day basis, we must be conscious of doing our own thinking. I have two beautiful parents whom I love so dearly; but, I don't love them enough to let them think for me. My husband—a man with whom I am so deeply in love and for whom I have endless admiration and respect; but not love, admiration, nor respect can convince me to let him do my thinking. I am blessed to have a terrific pastor who just excels in all areas of life and he means so much to me—but not enough to allow him to think for me. Why do I feel so strongly about this? Because I have learned the power and the fulfillment I experience when I exercise my right to think. The greatest Book ever written, the Bible, teaches me: "A man is as he thinketh." With that in mind, I want to be as I think, not as somebody else thinks.

One day as I was sitting in my living room meditating, I was overcome with this phrase: "I reserve the right to think for myself." As I began to put this affirmation into practice, I was bombarded with "opportunities to catch." Up until then, I had been content to let someone else determine my opportunities.

Once we decide to think for ourselves, even though no one will believe it, what happens next? I am convinced that making the decision to think for yourself or to catch the pearl is only the first step in a most exciting and extraordinary journey. It is extraordinary because you and I may be two of the few that have decided to travel this path. But the well-being, the accomplishments, the successes, and even the failures, contribute to making our trip through this world a practical "heaven on earth." As I found the beginning of this new philosophy a heavy challenge, I searched for my personal roadmap to doing my own thinking. As I began to develop this plan for my new excursion, I discovered a little word that I had known as a child.

This little four-letter word had been used on the school yard, out behind our small country church, and in other places (information I am not at liberty to divulge); but, then, I did not have the insight as to the explosive power from which I would personally profit once I understood its meaning as applied to my life. You, too, can experience this explosion in your life.

Dare!

All through my life, the word "Dare" has meant: to defy or to challenge with arrogance. But one afternoon, as I was flying from New Orleans to New York City to speak to a Parker Chiropractic Foundation Seminar at the Americana Hotel, I was consumed with a new definition of the word "Dare." I was ignited in all six areas of my life when I discovered this roadmap. From that moment until now, I am continuing to blaze with excitement, enthusiasm, and effectiveness, as I burn from a new source of fuel. It takes courage, and guts, and determination to think, to dare, to act, to catch your pearl. Is it worth it? Much more than words, or money, or position can ever express. That day, the word *dare* was redefined in my thinking and I am honored to share this roadmap with you.

Dare "D"—Develop a Confidence And a Commitment!

There is no feeling like that of believing in yourself. To know the strength that lies within your spirit is to know that you can think for yourself. Accept this fact: *Be yourself and become the best you can.* No one ever reaches a level of perfection; we are always continuing to strive to be a better person. God believed in me so much that He created me in the perfect image of love, of health, of prosperity, and I am confident that I am just exactly that. That attitude then makes me available to experience even greater health, wealth, love, etc. There is no substitute for a personal confidence in yourself. One of the major problems in our society in all age brackets, from children to senior citizens, is that we are not continuing to develop this imperative trait.

Once we begin developing our personal confidence, we must become committed to our thoughts, our actions, our philosophies. All down through history, men and women in all walks of life have been committed. Some of them should have been committed-committed; instead, they were strong leaders—some for the good and some for the not so good. To even begin the list, I risk not mentioning some of the great-greats; but I would like to share just a few who have had an over-bearing effect on me as I strive to "catch my pearl" every day.

Good Thinkers — Big Stinkers

We all are familiar with Adolf Hitler and how his confidence and commitment was imposed upon the lives of millions of people! How at the hand of one confident committed man, such a great disaster and destruction can occur. Then, on a much more positive note, we can vicariously share the life of a great woman like Helen Keller, who without speech, without sight, without hearing was confident that she could make a worthwhile contribution to her world. With that confidence came a commitment. When her friends and family seemingly discouraged her, she arose with greater courage and in her own special language proclaimed: "I can think for myself—make my own decisions and turn my liabilities into assets."

Every time we hop into an automobile, we get under the wheel of an invention from the mind of a man who was confident and committed. One of my favorite women who is an inspiration to us all is Rose Kennedy. Through tragedy after tragedy, her confidence and committment to life grew stronger. America needs confident and committed people whose goal is to make that worthwhile contribution.

The year 1978 brought a severe tragedy to the American public and peoples around the world. For once, we were able to see in action this acute deficiency of thinking for yourself. One person was able to lead hundreds of men and women and children to their death. Jim Jones thought for himself, but denied anyone else the right to do the same. Can we place the blame of Guyana on Jim Jones? No, I personally don't think so. Considering the fact that not any one of our institutions teaches the art of doing your own thinking, those who fell prey to his overbearing powers were victims (just like you and I could have been) of the greatest flaw in our philosophy. The heart-breaking fact is that the Jones scene can happen again. Only people who dare to think for themselves will prevent another Hitler or Jones! Only people who dare to be confident and committed will contribute valuable and beneficial input to our world. *Dare*—It takes courage, and guts, and determination to think, to dare, to act, to catch your pearl.

> Hey, I'm a believer now, since I had a change in my
>   mind.
> Hey, I'm a believer now and everything is gonna be
>   fine.
> Hey, I'm a believer now and everybody's going to see,
> Yes, I'm a believer now—I believe in me.
> Well, people think that I'm kind of strange
> Something's out of place.
> That big old frown I used to wear—
>   It's simply been erased.
> A smile has moved upon my face
> It stays there most of the time.
> My thinking is right—My living is great,
>   and I've become one of a kind.

Know thyself, Love thyself. Be open, be honest. Be you!
Practice these every day, this new habit we can do.
Our lives will change; Our worlds will grow
No, things won't be the same.
Since we've learned to love ourselves
We can better play this game.

Develop a confidence and a commitment.

Dare "A" —
Accept Your Responsibility!

At the time we are born, a shield of "She didn't mean to
do it" is placed around us. From that point on, we will grow
with the concept that we are not responsible for what we
say or do or become. Our words and deeds will always be
blamed on someone else or something else other than
ourselves. A child grows into a teenager, into a young
adult and on into adulthood blaming others for her lot in
life. As a child, I blamed my cousin, Brenda. As a teenager,
I blamed my best friend, Debbie. As a young adult, I
blamed the government. As an adult, I found myself blaming God. As a wife, I blamed my husband, and the list of
blames goes on and on.

Then, as I began to develop my personal system for
catching my pearls, I knew just as President Harry Truman knew when he said, "The buck stops here," and here
was with me! I strode into my dressing room and one of my
life changing events occurred. As I looked into that mirror
and saw the reflection of a "special" person, I determined
with all my heart, that never again would I blame someone else for my failure, or give someone else the credit for
my success. At that moment, I stood taller than I had ever
stood in my life; when you are only five feet tall, that is
some event. Not only did I stand taller, but I also stood
thinner. I dropped the excess baggage that I had been
carrying: mother, father, husband, God, government. I
had carried them with me everywhere I went so they
would be convenient when I needed them to accept my

responsibility. So to release them proved to be quite a weight reduction. After the mirror scene, I went to my study and picked up my Bible. It was there I read what God's will for my life really was. He wanted me to enjoy abundant life, health, and to prosper as my soul prospereth. I quietly said, "Dear God, forgive me for blaming you for the events that have happened in my life. All these years, I have misunderstood what your will for my life really was. Thank you for life, talent, ability, potential, and may I ever be conscious of my personal responsibility for *all* that happens to me." I cannot begin to tell you the changes, the opportunities, the excitement that began flooding my life.

To accept your responsibility is to dare to think for yourself. Yes, it takes courage; but, we must determine: "Do we really want to catch the pearl?"

A—Accept your responsibility.

Dare "R"— Research for Knowledge to Think for Yourself

When I determined that I really wanted to catch my pearls, I had to research for knowledge. Ignorance is not bliss; rather, ignorance is demeaning to the potential that lies between our ears, called the mind. People— everywhere I speak—love to be entertained; they accept being inspired, but strongly resist being informed. To learn is to live, and when we love to live we will love to learn. Learning ignites a "special" energy within the human body. This is the energy responsible for what we've come to tag as the "good things of life." When one begins to learn, one begins to think; then, one begins to act, and from this action all mankind will benefit. To think for yourself in all six areas of life (physical, mental, spiritual, social, financial, and family) requires varied information. To rightly decide our physical needs, we must know about diet, exercise, proper attire, vitamins, drugs, etc. If the women in the world who take Valium on a regular basis were informed properly about this drug, we all would break the mile record in staying away from it. But instead, we take whatever is prescribed for us with no knowledge whatsoever of its effects, and then blame the doctors for the results. It is our responsibility above that of the doctor to know what we put into our bodies.

A good friend of mine is an ardent smoker. I have talked with her on various occasions about this particular subject. After taking her much literature—both pro and con — on the subject, I was curious as to her decision. Of course, she thanked me for my concern and informed me that she had studied the information and consulted with her doctor. I immediately thought she had decided to quit. But to my aghast surprise, she said, "Zonnya, I have done my own thinking with the facts I have researched, and I have decided to continue my smoking." To this day, I have not mentioned it again. Once a person has done their homework, obtained facts, and made a decision based upon that research, then the responsibility of their research belongs to them. She was most happy with her thinking and with her decision. That is what makes doing your own thinking so beautiful and rewarding.

R—Research for knowledge to do your own thinking.

Dare "E"—Enjoy the Results of Doing Your Own Thinking

To dare to think for yourself will bring results much different from those results we experience when we allow others to think for us. Once I learned that either way — thinking for myself or others thinking for me—would always end in results, I determinedly decided to enjoy the results of my own thinking.

Much has been said and written about positive and negative thinking. I firmly believe that the third type of thinking has been underestimated. Our lives are under the auspices of three polarizations: positive, realistic, and negative. At a seminar in Tulsa, Oklahoma, following my presentation, an attractive business-looking woman approached me and asked if she could speak with me for just a moment. I affirmly responded and this is what she said,"Zonnya, I am a positive thinker and I practice the teachings and philosophy of optimism, but I am still plagued with problems and down situations. What am I doing wrong?" Having also felt this sense of helplessness, I was quite sympathetic to her dilemma. It was then that I differentiated the three poles of thinking that govern our lives. We have all experienced ups and downs, successes and failures. Furthermore, we all will continue to experience these mountain tops and valleys. Whatever the successes—whatever the failures, I prefer to experience them with me doing my own thinking, making my own decisions rather than with someone else doing it for me. To enjoy *my* results is to experience one faction of life that supercedes all others.

Dare "E"—Enjoy Your Results Of Doing Your Own Thinking

Yes, to dare to think for yourself requires self-love, self-determination, and self-confidence. Thinking always brings about the call to action. I coined this phrase that continues to encourage me in my thinking and acting: "*Thought* determines what you want; *action* determines what you get." To think for yourself moves one to act.

President Teddy Roosevelt, a man who dared to think for himself and then act upon his thoughts, transmitted a great message when he said:

"Far better it is to dare mighty things, to win glorious triumphs even though checkered by failure than to rank with those poor spirits who neither enjoy much nor suffer much because they live in that grey twilight that neither knows victory nor defeat."

When we dare and fulfill its hidden meaning, we can begin to experience the heightened euphoria of life. As we

continue our journeys through life, let us open our minds
to the boulevards of positive thinking. Let us eliminate
the dirt roads of negative thinking; but even more important, let us dare to function on the streets of realistic
thinking. That is what life is all about. With this philosophy, we can dare to think for ourselves, even though
nobody will believe it!

You may think it curious what I'm gonna say.
Think for yourself—Think for yourself.
Nobody really believes it when to them I say,
Think for yourself, you'll have a better day.

We tend to blame one another for what we do.
But that's unfair, yes so unfair.
We must understand that we're responsible
For every word and deed we must show care.

Yes, I know there is one thing that I must do.
I must accept my life as what I make it.
For there is no one outside of me to hold me back
Cause I'm doing my own thinking and that's a fact.

DO YOUR OWN THINKING—NOBODY WILL
BELIEVE IT!

WE KNOW YOU HAVE ENJOYED THESE STORIES OF OPPORTUNITY

Once a mind has been stretched with great ideas,
it can never return again to its former size.

WOULD YOU LIKE A SECOND HELPING?

AVAILABLE NOW!

No. 1 SUCCESS SECRETS! How 18 Everyday Women Became Builders and Famous Speakers! Role Models! Beautiful hardback. Stimulating, Inspirational, How to Build Your Business and Your Life.

Book
$11.95 ☐

No. 2 NEVER UNDERESTIMATE THE SELLING POWER OF A WOMAN by Dottie Walters. The FAMOUS best-seller, now out in paperback. The best sales book ever written by a woman for women in sales. Used as a textbook by many national Sales firms. Easy to read, full of power.

Book-Paperback
$ 4.95 ☐

No. 3 THE PEARL OF POTENTIALITY: Are You Ready to Catch It? An Anthology of women of Achievement. From a woman Train Engineer, to Inventors, to Speakers, a wealth of inspiration! Hardback, beautiful gift for women beginning their careers.

Book-Hardback
$11.95 ☐

No. 4 NEWSLETTER FOR SPEAKERS. How to set prices, get started, names of agents. A treasure for beginners and old-timers. A fortune to be made on the Platform! Six issues per year: $20.00

Newsletter
$20.00 ☐

No. 5	Big 6-hour CASSETTE ALBUM by Dottie Walters. Full course, Selling Power of a Woman — 6 cassettes — Dynamite	Cassette Album $59.00 ☐
No. 6	Cassette — 1 hour. Famous "7 SECRETS OF SELLING TO WOMEN!" by Dottie Walters (SMI)	Cassette-Single $ 9.95 ☐

AVAILABLE SOON

No. 7	Big 10 Cassette Album of the Famous Women in Success Secrets! Anthology on tape. 10 hours. Each Woman of Achievement tells her own story!	Cassette Album $69.00 ☐
No. 8	"WHAT DO YOU SAY TO AN AUDIENCE OF 10,000" Dottie Walters on Speaking. Single Cassette.	Cassette $ 9.95 ☐
No. 9	"IF YOU CAN DREAM IT, AND PLAN IT, YOU CAN DO IT!" Single cassette by Dottie Walters. This will lift you right out of your chair. Goal setting by the Champion!	Cassette $ 9.95 ☐

FREE WITH EACH ORDER: PARCHMENT COPY OF DOTTIE WALTERS' FAMOUS ANCIENT CHINESE SECRET, READY FOR FRAMING. BEAUTIFUL GIFT.

TAX DEDUCTIONS: An income tax deduction is allowed for expense of education (including registration, fee, meals, and lodging) undertaken to maintain and improve professional skills. (Treas. Reg. 1.162-5)

ORDER FORM

BOOKS				CASSETTES				NEWSLETTERS		
No.	Quantity	Amt.		No.	Quantity	Amt.		No.	Quantity	Amt.

Expiration Date

Ship To:

Total _____

Check Enclosed _____
Master Charge _____
Bankamericard _____
VISA _____
Acct. No. _____

Name _____

Address _____

City _____ State _____ Zip _____

Signature _____

Add 6% Sales Tax in Calif.
Plus $1.00 Shipping and handling per item.
$2.00 out of the U.S.A.
American Currency only.
$20.00 Min. on charge card orders (M.C. or VISA)

Make Checks Payable to: ROYAL CBS PUBLISHING, 600 W. Foothill Blvd., Glendora, CA 91740

March Fong Eu's Delightful Fairy Tale SONS OF CHONG may be obtained from
CAREER PUBLISHING, INC., 924 N. Main Street, P.O. Box 5486, Orange
California 92667 — (714) 997-0130 — Price: $6.95 plus $1.25 shipping and handling.

ORDER FORM

BOOKS				CASSETTES				NEWSLETTERS		
No.	Quantity	Amt.		No.	Quantity	Amt.		No.	Quantity	Amt.

Expiration Date

Check Enclosed _____
Master Charge _____
Bankamericard _____
VISA _____
Acct. No. _____

Ship To:

Name _____

Address _____

City _____ State _____ Zip _____

Signature _____

Total _____

Add 6% Sales Tax in Calif.
Plus $1.00 Shipping and handling per item.
$2.00 out of the U.S.A.
American Currency only.
$20.00 Min. on charge card orders (M.C. or VISA)

Make Checks Payable to: ROYAL CBS PUBLISHING, 600 W. Foothill Blvd., Glendora, CA 91740

March Fong Eu's Delightful Fairy Tale SONS OF CHONG may be obtained from
CAREER PUBLISHING, INC., 924 N. Main Street, P.O. Box 5486, Orange
California 92667 — (714) 997-0130 — Price: $6.95 plus $1.25 shipping and handling.